W9-BJB-200

Issues in Immigration

Other books in the Contemporary Issues series:

Issues in Alcohol
Issues in Biomedical Ethics
Issues in Censorship
Issues in Crime
Issues in the Environment
Issues in the Information Age
Issues in Racism
Issues in Sports

CONTEMPORARY ISSUES

Issues in Immigration

by Stephen Currie

Lucent Books, San Diego, CA

Library of Congress Cataloging-in-Publication Data

Currie, Stephen, 1960–
    Issues in immigration / by Stephen Currie.
       p. cm.—(Contemporary issues)
    Includes bibliographical references and index.
    Summary: Discusses various issues regarding immigration, including assimilation, jobs, services, illegal immigration, and policy.
    ISBN 1-56006-377-7 (lib. bdg. : alk. paper)
    1. United States—Emigration and immigration—Juvenile literature.
[1. United States—Emigration and immigration.] I. Title. II.
Contemporary issues (San Diego, Calif.)

JV6465.C87   2000
325.73—dc21   99-088268

TABLE OF CONTENTS

Foreword 6

Introduction
A Nation of Immigrants 9

Chapter 1
Should Assimilation Be a Priority for
Immigrants? 13
Chapter 2
Does Immigration Harm U.S. Workers? 30
Chapter 3
Should Immigrants Be Denied Access
to Government Services? 44
Chapter 4
Should Efforts to Halt Illegal Immigration
Be Strengthened? 56
Chapter 5
Should Immigration Policy Be Reformed? 74

Notes 91

Organizations to Contact 97

For Further Reading 99

Works Consulted 101

Index 106

Picture Credits 111

About the Author 112

Foreword

When men are brought face to face with their opponents, forced to listen and learn and mend their ideas, they cease to be children and savages and begin to live like civilized men. Then only is freedom a reality, when men may voice their opinions because they must examine their opinions.

Walter Lippmann, American editor and writer

CONTROVERSY FOSTERS DEBATE. The very mention of a controversial issue prompts listeners to choose sides and offer opinions. But seeing beyond one's opinions is often difficult. As Walter Lippmann implies, true reasoning comes from the ability to appreciate and understand a multiplicity of viewpoints. This ability to assess the range of opinions is not innate; it is learned by the careful study of an issue. Those who wish to reason well, as Lippmann attests, must be willing to examine their own opinions even as they weigh the positive and negative qualities of the opinions of others.

The *Contemporary Issues* series explores controversial topics through the lens of opinion. The series addresses some of today's most debated issues and, drawing on the diversity of opinions, presents a narrative that reflects the controversy surrounding those issues. All of the quoted testimonies are taken from primary sources and represent both prominent and lesser-known persons who have argued these topics. For example, the title on biomedical ethics contains the views of physicians commenting on both sides of the physician-assisted suicide issue: Some wage a moral argument that assisted suicide allows patients to die with dignity, while others assert that assisted suicide violates the Hippocratic oath. Yet the book also includes the opinions of those who see the issue in a more personal way. The relative of a person who died by assisted suicide feels the loss of a loved one and makes a plaintive cry against it, while companions of another assisted suicide victim attest that their friend no longer wanted to endure the agony of a slow death. The profusion of quotes illustrates the range of thoughts and emotions that impinge on any debate. Displaying the range of perspectives, the series is designed to show how personal belief—whether informed by statistical evidence, religious conviction, or public opinion—shapes and complicates arguments.

Each title in the *Contemporary Issues* series discusses multiple controversies within a single field of debate. The title on environmental issues, for example, contains one chapter that asks whether the Endangered Species Act should be repealed, while another asks if Americans can afford the economic and social costs of environmentalism. Narrowing the focus of debate to a specific question, each chapter sharpens the competing perspectives and investigates the philosophies and personal convictions that inform these viewpoints.

Students researching contemporary issues will find this format particularly useful in uncovering the central controversies of topics by placing them in a moral, economic, or political context that allows the students to easily see the points of disagreement. Because of this structure, the series provides an excellent launching point for further research. By clearly defining major points of contention, the series also aids readers in critically examining the structure and source of debates. While providing a resource on which to model persuasive essays, the quoted opinions also permit students to investigate the credibility and usefulness of the evidence presented.

For students contending with current issues, the ability to assess the credibility, usefulness, and persuasiveness of the testimony as well as the factual evidence given by the quoted experts is critical not only in judging the merits of these arguments but in analyzing the students' own beliefs. By plumbing the logic of another person's opinions, readers will be better able to assess their own thinking. And this, in turn, can promote the type of introspection that leads to a conviction based on reason. Though *Contemporary Issues* offers the opportunity to shape one's own opinions in light of competing or concordant philosophies, above all, it shows readers that well-reasoned, well-intentioned arguments can be countered by opposing opinions of equal worth.

Critically examining one's own opinions as well as the opinions of others is what Walter Lippmann believes makes an individual "civilized." Developing the skill early can only aid a reader's understanding of both moral conviction and political action. For students, a facility for reasoning is indispensable. Comprehending the foundations of opinions leads the student to the heart of controversy—to a recognition of what is at stake when holding a certain viewpoint. But the goal is not detached analysis; the issues are often far too immediate for that. The *Contemporary Issues* series induces the reader not only to see the shape of a current controversy, but to engage it, to respond to it, and ultimately to find one's place within it.

A Nation of Immigrants

THE UNITED STATES IS OFTEN called a nation of immigrants, with good reason. Except for a handful of people of pure Native American ancestry, every American living today has ancestors who arrived in this country at most five hundred years ago—and in most cases much more recently than that. Some, notably Africans brought to the New World as slaves, did not come here willingly. But the majority of newcomers to this nation have been immigrants by choice. Over the centuries, the United States has attracted millions of people eager for a better life in a new land.

Today, the influx continues at near-record levels. During each year of the 1990s, between 800,000 and 900,000 foreigners entered the United States with the intention of staying—and that number includes only those who arrived legally. The current annual level of

Immigrants, hoping for opportunity in the United States, gather inside the Immigrant Building on Ellis Island.

illegal immigration is estimated at perhaps another 300,000 persons. Taken together, well over a million immigrants enter the United States every year.

Reasons

The recent high level of immigration is due to several factors. One of the most obvious is the loosening of certain official restrictions on immigration. Between the early 1920s and the 1980s, U.S. policy placed strict limits on the number of immigrants permitted. The total number of immigrants allowed entry was much lower than it is today. Moreover, the quota system used at the time reserved many of those spots for Western Europeans—and by the middle of the twentieth century, relatively few Irish, German, or English nationals were interested in emigrating. Thus, a large number of the available slots went unused, further reducing total immigration.

More recently, however, limits have been raised. There are now more slots open to would-be immigrants than at any point since the early 1920s. At the same time, national quotas have been eliminated, thus ensuring that nearly all available places will be filled. Of course, today's laws do not permit unlimited numbers of immigrants: Many people who long to settle in the United States are turned away every year. Nevertheless, changes in the laws have extended admission to many people who would never have qualified as immigrants under the old rules.

There are other reasons for the recent wave of immigration. The end of the twentieth century has seen more than its share of wars, political dislocation, and economic hardship. Each so-called push factor has resulted in a stream of people desperate to enter the relatively safe and stable United States The 1990s also has been a decade of steady economic growth within the United States, and immigrants are more likely to leave their homes when they can expect jobs. Another so-called pull factor is that American businesses are becoming much more aggressive in seeking out workers from abroad. Likewise, as the world's economies become increasingly interconnected, would-be immigrants are more likely than ever to know about job opportunities in the United States—and to have the wherewithal to go after them.

Haitian refugees sail to the United States. The economic growth of the United States is one reason for the recent wave of immigration.

Controversy

The recent high level of immigration is highly controversial, however. The debate rages on many fronts, but a chief focus is the effect of immigration on the United States. Some thinkers fear that the nation will be fragmented and overwhelmed by alien cultures, by people who will insist on keeping their own separate ethnic identity rather than becoming recognizably "American." Others worry that immigrants take jobs away from native-born workers, or that they use more than their fair share of taxpayer resources. All these concerns reflect their adherents' image of America today: a nation in danger of being undermined by immigration, both culturally and economically. It comes as no surprise that most of these thinkers would like to restrict or even eliminate immigration in the future.

To each of these arguments, of course, there is a counter-argument. Immigrants *do* assimilate into American society, some experts say, even if assimilation today differs from the way immigrants joined American society fifty or a hundred years ago. Immigrant labor, some assert, actually expands the economy. Others claim that immigrants contribute much more in taxes than they get in benefits. To these thinkers, America is enriched, both culturally and economically, by the presence of immigrants, and should continue to be so.

This, then, is the backdrop for the debates on immigration that follow. The central question for a self-described "nation of immigrants" is, indeed, how current levels of immigration affect the nation. Some argue that immigration is entirely good for the country; others say it is all bad. The truth may actually be in the middle: Certain aspects of immigration policy are helpful to the country and should be continued, while others are less helpful, even harmful, and should be changed. But in the end, agreeing on answers may be less important than simply asking the questions. The answers depend not only on the facts of immigration, but also on each person's individual vision of the United States; the questions, however, provoke responses from us all.

Chapter 1

Should Assimilation Be a Priority for Immigrants?

IN THE SUMMER OF 1999, the city council of El Cenizo, Texas, passed an ordinance that created a national stir. All city government business, the new law stated, was to be conducted in Spanish. Any resident of El Cenizo was entitled to English translations of debates, proceedings, or documents after a forty-eight-hour wait. However, the effect of the law was clear: Officially, Spanish would take precedence over English. In the conduct of government, Spanish was to be the main language.

The Balkanization of America

The new law created a storm of controversy outside El Cenizo, a South Texas community whose seventy-five hundred residents are nearly all Mexican by birth or parentage. Many observers saw a political statement in the ruling—an attempt to separate El Cenizo from the rest of the United States. In this view, the city council's decision served to help townspeople keep their Mexican identity. Rather than buy into American culture, traditions, and language, these observers charged, El Cenizans were trying to live in the United States without choosing to be fully a part of it. "They don't really consider themselves American," sums up Tim Schultz of US English, a group established to promote the use of English as the nation's only official language.[1]

Schultz is not alone in protesting the Texas ordinance. Most who agree with him oppose the law because of its potential negative effect on the United States. "This portends what more and more communities are going to look like," says immigration reform advocate John

13

Keeley.[2] Opponents of the law foresee political fragmentation as sections of the country reject English for the languages of various recent immigrant groups. "The Balkanization [breaking up] of America along linguistic lines," Schultz calls it, envisioning areas where English has been officially rejected in favor of Spanish, Korean, Chinese, Portuguese, and a sea of other languages.[3]

Worse, opponents fear, the rejection of English could turn into a wholesale rejection of American culture and value systems. Instead of assimilating—that is, adopting traditional American ideals and ways of life—newly arrived immigrants would continue to follow the customs and mores of their home nation, ignoring dearly held practices and conventions. Some experts argue that the current form, even the basic existence, of the United States is threatened by rulings like El Cenizo's, which permit and even encourage immigrants to remain separate—linguistically and culturally—from their new neighbors.

"Not Everyone Can Speak English"

But most El Cenizans dismiss this argument. In support of the new law, El Cenizo officials point to the town's demographics: About three-quarters of the population speak only Spanish. Far from being a political statement, they assert, the law simply reflects the realities of life along the border. Officials argue that a good, responsive government ought to use the language that people are most comfortable speaking. "The idea is to communicate with the people," says Mayor Rafael Rodriguez. "When the meetings were in English, that didn't happen."[4] And in fact, the new measure was roundly approved by the town's citizens.

Nor do town residents see themselves as antiassimilation. Although "almost everyone speaks Spanish in El Cenizo," says city commissioner Flora Barton, "that doesn't mean that we want to be Mexican or go become a part of Mexico. We're proud to be American."[5] English is taught in the schools, proponents of the law point out, and many adults take English lessons at community centers. Within two or three generations, El Cenizo residents will likely be as fluent in English as in Spanish.

Moreover, some observers believe that the El Cenizo move, by encouraging immigrant participation in government, actually helps

Children rollerblade in the city of El Cenizo, Texas. The city council of El Cenizo enacted a controversial law that all city government business was to be conducted in Spanish.

the cause of assimilation. "Not everyone can speak English," points out a Los Angeles attorney who works on Mexican American issues. "They shouldn't be locked out of government just because they're in the process of learning it."[6] By giving people a stake in their government, this argument runs, the Spanish-first law encourages immigrants to get involved and to be aware of what is happening in their new country.

The ultimate effect of El Cenizo's decision is anyone's guess. The law may have the effect of distancing El Cenizans from the rest of the United States, as one side fears, or it may actually help bring the town closer to the mainstream of American life. Whatever happens, El Cenizo will continue to be a flashpoint in the debate over assimilation of immigrants.

Assimilation

The issue of assimilation lies close to the heart of American identity. Americans have traditionally believed that immigrants can and should be gradually brought into the mainstream of national life. This perspective is so fundamental in the United States that many Americans are surprised to find that very few other countries share it.

Instead, most other nations follow one of two models. In the first, common in countries with one dominant ethnic group, such as France or Italy, outsiders are never fully accepted as members of the community. "With very few exceptions," writes an immigration expert, "you can only be a German if your ancestors were German. There are hundreds of thousands of second and third generations of people, born in Germany, knowing no other nation, who are not German, who never will be German."[7] In these nations, assimilation as Americans know it is an alien concept. People born outside the dominant culture cannot move into it in any meaningful way.

The second model is common in multiethnic countries such as Belgium, Russia, or the former Yugoslavia. In these places, there is little sense of shared culture. Instead, two or more religious, ethnic, or cultural groups exist more or less tensely side by side. Many nations that follow this model have eventually broken apart violently or have suffered long-term civil wars. Even those which have avoided violence are held together under pressure. Indeed, as author Peter D. Salins argues, "All the nations that have ever embraced [this model] have had to live with perpetual ethnic discord."[8]

The United States has traditionally rejected both these models. In the United States, new residents are expected to make their way into the dominant culture, with full rights and responsibilities as members of the group. Any ethnicity can be accommodated. As author Francis Fukuyama puts it, "To be an American has meant to be committed to a certain set of ideas, and not to be descended from an original tribe of *ur* [original] Americans."[9] The American way of assimilation, supporters reason, gives all Americans a common cultural perspective, a way of looking at the world which can be shared by Americans of Mexican, Korean, and Polish descent. In this view, the people of the United States are no longer Irish, or Indian, or Dominican, but instead distinctively American.

Ethnic Albanians attend the reburial of Albanians who were killed in a Serb offensive. Ethnic fighting is common in countries that lack a sense of shared culture.

History

The emphasis on assimilation has deep roots in American history. Throughout the nineteenth and early twentieth centuries the United States took in waves of immigrants, expecting that they would sooner or later adopt American customs, speech, and ways of life. Indeed, for most native-born Americans, assimilation was an unquestioned fact. Those who refused to adopt American cultural traditions and values were not wanted. "Every immigrant who comes here," suggested Theodore Roosevelt in 1918, "should be required within five years to learn English or leave the country." [10]

While five years was not always enough time, there is no doubt that in the long run the assimilationist ethic prevailed. If immigrants themselves did not learn English, their children and grandchildren did. Today, their descendants are more or less indistinguishable from one another. Though many of them prize and celebrate their ethnic roots, nearly all have become thoroughly "American." The great-grandchildren of nineteenth-century arrivals from Germany, with few exceptions, no longer speak German. In the same way, fourth-generation Italian Americans have little in common with present-day Romans, and a teenager whose ancestors left China for the United States a century ago would be much more at home in any American city than in Shanghai.

Over the years, Americans have celebrated their nation's ability to blend many cultures into one. "Celt and Latin, Slav and Teuton, Greek and Syrian, black and yellow . . . Jew and Gentile," wrote playwright Israel Zangwill in 1908. "Here shall they all unite to build the Republic of Man and the Kingdom of God."[11] Zangwill's words were highly romantic, but the power of his vision for Americans of his time is undeniable. Many citizens truly believed that assimilation would take place, and that this newly forged culture would make a more ideal world. Even today, Zangwill's philosophy lives on, in assimilationist ideals as well as in the phrase he coined in the title of his most famous play, *The Melting Pot*—a phrase adopted to describe the merging of cultures that has traditionally marked America.

Unassimilated Immigrants

But in recent years many experts have detected changes in America's assimilationist ethic. Commentator and political candidate Patrick Buchanan sums up the concern in one sentence: "The great American Melting Pot is not melting, as once it did."[12] Increasingly, Buchanan believes, immigrants are unwilling to give up cherished traditions or ethnic identity in exchange for full participation in American life. Not only that, some fear that the United States itself no longer demands—or even asks—that immigrants do so.

According to this view, rather than being absorbed into the mainstream of American society, immigrants are allowed to live in the United States while remaining distinctively ethnic, even foreign. The result, Buchanan and others believe, will be chaos. In one scenario, unassimilated immigrants and their descendants will change

Many immigrants, including these Chinese people celebrating the Chinese New Year, believe it is important to retain their culture.

the face of America through sheer numbers and the power of their culture. "A country which in 2050 will be, for example, one-quarter Latino," warns immigration reformer Peter Brimelow, "must also be, in some degree, Latin American in its politics and culture." [13]

A slightly different perspective presupposes an eventual split between immigrants and native-born Americans. Culturally and linguistically, immigrants will dominate certain parts of the nation. The shared experiences and perspectives that have always marked America will fade, to be replaced by aggressively ethnic viewpoints in conflict with what the United States has traditionally stood for. At best the United States will become another Canada or Belgium, torn between two or more competing ethnic groups. At worst it will be torn into bits by violence, as has been the case in Lebanon or Yugoslavia. In either case, the transformation will be dramatic.

Rejection

No one denies that some immigrants simply do not wish to assimilate. Some people plan to spend only a few years living and working in the United States. Since they intend to return to their homelands, they

Many members of New York's Dominican community remain devoted to their country and desire to return home after achieving success in America.

have no incentive to adopt their neighbors' values and customs. New York City's Dominican community is one example. "A disturbingly large number of Dominicans see New York and America as only a temporary way station—a place to make some money," charges Peter Salins. "In the meantime, they constantly travel back and forth, undermining the assimilationist order." [14]

Short-term immigrants are not the only ones who reject the goal of assimilation. Some immigrant leaders adopt a deliberately anti-assimilation stance, encouraging others from their homelands to join them in preserving cultural and social mores. A popular poem by Mexican immigrant Rodolfo Gonzales boasts, "I will never be absorbed." [15] This process of reverse assimilation, in which the immigrant culture, not the native version, proves dominant, is a favorite theme of some immigrant leaders. Men and women from Mexico, argues writer Carlos Loret de Mola, "continue to be Mexican and even . . . impress their personality on their surroundings." [16]

To those who fear that the United States is in danger of breaking up into ethnic factions, rhetoric like this is alarming indeed. Strong believers in assimilation frequently cite the more radical activists—and the admittedly short-term migrants—in support of the notion that something is going wrong. But proassimilationists do not simply base their case on the actions of a few Dominicans or a handful of Mexican American activists. The Buchanans and Brimelows voice more general concerns related both to immigrants themselves and to the American response to them.

Increasingly, proassimilationists argue, immigrants are adopting an aggressive stance against the melting pot. Rather than take on American values and customs as most immigrants did two or three generations ago, today's immigrants are far more likely to reject the American way of life, with dangerous consequences for the nation as a whole. Much of the blame, according to this perspective, lies with the immigrants themselves, but a large share of it can be traced to native-born Americans who coddle newcomers instead of insisting that they assimilate as quickly as possible.

Language

Some of these changes involve the growing prevalence of languages other than English in America today. While El Cenizo is—at least at present—a special case, the trend has certainly been toward greater tolerance and acceptance of Spanish, Chinese, and other languages brought to the United States by immigrants. The voice mail systems of an increasing number of U.S. companies routinely ask the user's preference for English or Spanish. Many American cities have radio and television stations broadcasting exclusively in foreign languages, and churches serving high-density immigrant populations frequently offer religious services in languages other than English.

Of greater concern to advocates of assimilation, however, are the public policy decisions which promote communication in languages other than English. Many city governments today print brochures and official publications in several languages, a move virtually unheard-of a few decades ago. Printed material includes basic information critical for citizenship proceedings, passing employment tests, obtaining driver licenses, and even voting. Several large cities also hire interpreters at council meetings upon request, and at least five Los Angeles County municipalities provide them as a matter of course.

Similarly, school systems now incorporate many languages besides English. The Hamtramck, Michigan, school district sends home memos in Arabic, Bengali, Serbo-Croatian, and four other languages. Bilingual education programs have been a staple of public school curriculums across America for more than a generation. In these programs, students are taught at least partly in the language they know best. Columnist Linda Chavez, an opponent of this practice, argues that bilingual education has a political and antiassimilationist effect: It is "at its heart a program to help maintain the language and culture of [immigrant] children."[17]

A teacher gives an American history lesson to her bilingual class.

Culture and Values

Language, however, is far from the only concern. Many observers believe that immigrants' values and cultural backgrounds are too often at odds with those of native-born Americans. This is especially true today, when immigrants increasingly come from developing nations in Asia, Africa, and Latin America with traditions not at all like those of native-born Americans. As Brimelow writes, "Immigrants from developed countries assimilate better than those from underdeveloped countries."[18]

Certainly newcomers' cultural reference points are frequently different from those of people who have lived here for years. In one instance, the Hamtramck schools had to give up a long-standing tradition in which students gave friends carnations on Valentine's Day. The tradition "was misinterpreted by some recent immigrants," reports a journalist, "who wondered whether their daughters were now engaged."[19]

More troublesome than Valentine's Day traditions, however, are customs pertaining to family life. The Hmong people of Laos, many of whom immigrated to Minnesota, Wisconsin, and California following the Vietnam War in the late 1970s, have frequently been singled out for their drastically different customs. Traditional Hmong culture, for instance, calls for physical beatings of children who misbehave. Transplanted to America, this custom has had serious consequences. "The parents try to discipline [their children] like they did back in the old country," notes a chief of police, "but if they bruise their kids, we arrest them for child abuse. And the parents can't comprehend it."[20]

Similarly, the Hmong have come under attack for customs regarding medical care and marriage. "Hmong with epilepsy are revered as healers, a people who are spiritually distinguished rather than ill," explains a reporter. "So Hmong parents routinely deny medical care to their epileptic children."[21] But U.S. doctors, like most native-born Americans, see epilepsy as a disorder that can—and should—be treated medically. As for marriage, Hmong tradition dictates that girls marry in their early teens. "These traditional practices are just not acceptable here," concedes a Hmong journalist— yet the Hmong continue to follow their roots.[22]

Hmong women celebrate the Hmong New Year. Sometimes the cultural beliefs and practices of immigrant groups such as the Hmong can be in conflict with the dominant culture and legal system of their adopted land.

The Hmong are not the only immigrant group accused of holding too tightly to tradition. "Many recent arrivals from Mexico and Central America are now resisting assimilation," a Southern California priest reports. "American holidays are scorned, yet 'Cinco de Mayo' and Mexican Independence Day inspire major celebrations."[23] Others charge that Chinese, Russian, or Jamaican immigrants are not adopting American culture quickly enough. A Minnesota disc jockey demanded on air that the Hmong "either assimilate or hit the . . . road"; a sizable group of Americans agree with him, whether about the Hmong or about any of the other ethnic groups that make up America's immigrants today.[24]

Changing American Culture

Many other native-born Americans, however, deny that assimilation is a problem. In fact, some believe that the United States is strengthened, not weakened, by immigrants who adhere to old customs and values. The United States, they point out, has been built on many different traditions. As Salins writes, "African-American, Hispanic, Jewish, Italian, Asian, and other ethnic influences are now deeply and ineradicably embedded in the national cultural mix, and new ethnic influences are changing that mix every day."[25]

In this view, immigrants do not simply "become" assimilated; rather, they subtly change American culture themselves as they learn new American ways. "Assimilation has always been a two-way process," says a British writer, "with each new wave of immigrants contributing something to what it means to be American, from Jewish humour to German beer."[26] The result is a dynamic, ever-changing national culture, able to shift with the times, not a hidebound, static, and inflexible society such as many Americans see in European countries.

Moreover, assimilation has never been as easy as some believe. While assimilation has worked in the long run, in the short run it has been complicated and cumbersome. Throughout history, one journalist points out, immigrants have been "stereotyped as eternal foreigners, unwilling to assimilate and endlessly posing a threat to American culture."[27] Just as is true today, the reasons have had something to do with immigrants themselves and something to do with the attitudes of native-born Americans.

Historically, some immigrant groups were not permitted to assimilate. Anti-Asian prejudice in the late nineteenth century sentenced many Chinese immigrants to substandard housing and menial jobs. In New York, says one writer, "many landlords preferred to let their buildings sit idle rather than rent them to men who wore 'pigtails.'"[28] Barred from participation in American society, it is no wonder that Chinese immigrants kept their traditional hairstyles, along with traditional clothing, language, and foods. The process of assimilation for these Chinese and their descendants took several decades, a far cry from the five years that Theodore Roosevelt suggested.

Others did not want to assimilate. The Dominicans of turn-of-the-millennium New York are quite similar to the Italians who arrived in New York a century earlier. Nearly half the Italian immigrants during that time chose to return home as soon as they could afford to. Whether their temporary presence in the United States had a long-term negative impact on American values is doubtful.

An Italian immigrant family poses for a picture at Ellis Island. Italian immigrants who came to America in the early 1900s resisted assimilation.

And still others simply did not assimilate. Just as Spanish functions today as an unofficial language across the Southwest, so was German widespread throughout much of the central United States during the nineteenth century. Settling near friends and relatives from Europe, Germans formed enclaves in which their own language, traditions, and customs took precedence. As late as World War I, visitors to certain midwestern cities were better off speaking

German than English. "Germany," wrote an editorialist in 1914, "seems to have lost all of her foreign possessions with the exception of Milwaukee, St. Louis, and Cincinnati."[29] Again, the overall cause of assimilation was not harmed.

Immigrants Today

But the strongest challenges to the notion that assimilation is not working come from studies of today's immigrants themselves. The situation in El Cenizo notwithstanding, only about 8 percent of all immigrants speak no English. Within ten years of arrival, about three-quarters speak English "with high proficiency."[30] And immigrants themselves overwhelmingly see mastering English as a valuable skill. One study found that 90 percent of Hispanic Americans say that all residents of the United States ought to learn English, a statistic that suggests a strong desire to assimilate.

This trend is especially true among children. According to one study, four-fifths of South Florida immigrants prefer English to their parents' native languages. According to another, 95 percent of the children of Mexican immigrants speak excellent English. A third study indicates that half of all Asian immigrant children speak no language but English. "Slowly, often painfully, but quite assuredly," writes a researcher, today's immigrants "embrace the cultural norms that are part of life in the United States."[31]

Certainly many immigrants speak eagerly of blending in. "People say I have hardly a trace of the Irish accent," says a New York woman who grew up in Ireland, "and that makes me very happy."[32] Others share typical American dreams and values. Home ownership is one; many Americans know immigrants like the nursing assistant from Jamaica who saved for years to buy a house in the Washington suburbs. Family life is another. "He will be a kind and responsible husband and father," predicts a columnist about a man from Cameroon. "His family will be an example of 'family values,' albeit perhaps very different in aspect from the mental picture of those so quick to tout those values."[33] And hard work is a third. The industry of Korean grocers in California, Vietnamese fishermen in Texas, and Mexican restaurant workers in upstate New York sometimes "out-Americans" Americans.

"They Will Become Americans"

In the debate over assimilation, the two sides see the controversy from very different perspectives, choosing to highlight certain facts and figures and playing down others. To some, the action of the El Cenizo city council is a sign of impending disaster. To others, it is outweighed by polls showing the desire of immigrants to assimilate and the historical evidence that immigration has never been easy. To some, the prevalence of so-called reverse assimilation is an indication that American culture is flexible, while others fear that the process will destroy the nation.

Immigrants take their oath of citizenship. Immigration advocates argue that assimilation of immigrants into the predominant American culture, while sometimes slow, is inevitable.

But most Americans do agree that assimilation is a worthy goal, even if they disagree on how it should be achieved and on how long the process should take. And many Americans do believe that assimilation will continue. Among these optimists is author Bill Bryson, who writes,

> If history is anything to go by, then three things about America's immigrants are as certain today as they ever were: that they will learn English, that they will become Americans, and that the country will be stronger for it. And if that is not a good thing, I don't know what is.[34]

Chapter 2

Does Immigration Harm U.S. Workers?

D URING THE MIDDLE OF THE twentieth century, the large meat-packing companies of the American Midwest employed thousands of workers. Overwhelmingly white and native born, these blue-collar workers settled in cities like Omaha and Kansas City as well as in smaller towns, and many did well. Quite a few meatpackers owned their own homes and sent their children to college, and a strong union made sure that wages and job security were good. "I never had seen such paychecks in my life," recalls a man who joined a company in Storm Lake, Iowa, in 1959.[35]

True, meatpacking was a messy and dangerous industry. On the cutting floor, men with sharp knives carved up one animal carcass after another with barely a pause. Blood and entrails frequently covered the room, and the "constantly clanging machinery and chilly temperatures" were further distractions.[36] Cuts and falls serious enough to require medical attention were common. But the unions helped eliminate some of the most dangerous safety issues, and in any case the workers were well enough paid to live with a little risk.

The meatpacking plants still operate in Minnesota, Iowa, and other midwestern states, especially in the smaller cities and towns. Since 1980, however, the meat processing industry has changed. By all accounts, it is an increasingly dangerous occupation. The work is messier, too, and the pace is more frenetic than ever: "Carcasses whiz by at four hundred or more an hour," writes a researcher.[37]

But perhaps the most obvious change involves the workforce. Middle-class white meatpackers are a dying breed. Over the years,

A meatpacker inspects slaughtered hogs. Wages in meat processing plants have declined dramatically as native-born, middle-class meatpackers have been replaced by immigrant laborers.

companies have replaced the native-born processors with immigrants from Mexico, Somalia, Laos, and other countries. In some factories, scarcely any native-born Americans remain. In others, the number of natives drops consistently. More and more, immigrants are filling jobs formerly held by those born and raised in the United States.

At the same time, wages have plummeted. The Iowa Beef Processors plant in Storm Lake, for instance, now pays its employees an average hourly wage of $7—a far cry from the $19 workers in 1980 took home. Benefits have shrunk, too. Those companies offering health insurance typically require a six-month waiting period, meaning that any injuries incurred during that time are solely the responsibility of the employee.

Controversy

The use of immigrant meatpackers has become extremely controversial for a number of reasons. Some worry that the migrants are
being exploited. Stories abound of immigrants being forced out of
their jobs shortly before they become eligible for benefits or raises;
intimidated into accepting company doctors' opinions that they are
healthy enough to work; and fired simply for asking whether rest
periods could be lengthened. Others fear the influx of so many
unskilled, uneducated immigrants into the small towns where meatpacking companies set up factories. Towns such as Garden City,
Kansas, and Lexington, Nebraska, have seen crime, poverty, and
child abuse soar after meatpacking concerns brought in immigrants.
The stresses and dislocations are harmful to immigrants and the
native born alike.

But perhaps the biggest controversy regarding the immigrant
meat processors involves jobs. The transition from middle-class
white employees to immigrants was not an easy one. During the
1980s, the industry suffered bitter strikes and controversial layoffs;
companies went bankrupt, then opened up again under different
names, often replacing virtually the entire workforce in the process.
Unions were squeezed out, and company officials began openly
searching for immigrants to work on the cutting floors. Iowa Beef,
a journalist reports, "has consistently used labor brokers to comb the
border areas in south Texas and California to shuttle up new recruits
at as much as $300 a head." [38]

The factories' actions lead to a tricky ethical question. In one
view, U.S. citizens have lost their jobs in the meatpacking industry
simply because they could be replaced by Third World immigrants
willing to work for less. "The use of immigrants," says an Iowa his-
torian, "was a blatant and obvious attempt to undercut the labor
movement." [39] That formulation worries a good many observers.
According to this perspective, the meatpacking plants should never
have had the option of hiring so many low-wage immigrants. The
possibility of doing so has led to widespread dislocation among
American workers and a clear reduction in their standard of living.

Others disagree. While not necessarily approving the industry's
actions, they do not believe that immigrant hiring was the problem.

In the 1980s, bitter strikes such as this one and controversial layoffs caused many meat processing companies to go bankrupt.

Reduced demand for meat and more global competition led to a crisis in the industry, they argue; wages were bound to decline and layoffs to increase. Furthermore, they say, changes in production methods have considerably altered the industry since the late 1970s. The work is now too messy, dangerous, and strenuous for most American citizens. "There are jobs that native-born Americans simply won't do," says a Kansas job placement specialist. "Meatpacking is one of them."[40]

In one sense, the meatpacking controversy has been resolved. For the foreseeable future, the percentage of immigrant workers on the cutting floors will continue to rise each year. There is no going back to the 1960s. But in another sense, the debate continues to rage. The meatpacking industry is far from the only one in America replacing native-born workers with immigrants. The morality of doing so, and the effect on the country as a whole, remain compelling and important issues.

Anti-Immigrant Sentiment

The debate regarding jobs and immigrants is complex and often heated. To many Americans, the evidence is clear: High levels of immigration hurt U.S. citizens in the job market. Because the number of jobs available in this country is finite, every immigrant who takes a job is technically either throwing a native-born American out of work or blocking the hiring of an unemployed citizen. The effect of this is seen at all levels of American society, but most clearly among the poor: "It is not mere coincidence that the unemployment crisis of the inner cities has intensified with the massive increase of unskilled immigrants," warns commentator Ronald Steel.[41]

Many Americans are drawn to this equation: Immigrants seek and hold jobs, while some percentage of American citizens is unemployed. When numbers in either group grow large, it is hard to escape the conclusion that the one causes the other. High immigration rates therefore strike many Americans as unfair and harmful— harmful to the American workers, and by extension harmful to the entire United States. "At a time when unemployment is at a record high," said an Urban League official in 1983, "it is difficult to stand up and cheer these new citizens."[42]

Indeed, Americans may find it hard to "cheer these new citizens" even in recent years, when unemployment rates have been relatively low. Meatpacking is not the only industry which has moved from almost exclusive use of native-born workers to an equally heavy reliance on immigrants. Once mostly filled by African Americans, for instance, building maintenance jobs in Los Angeles are mainly held today by immigrants from Mexico. Similarly, Houston construction crews, according to a recent study, are now nearly one-third immigrant. And this process is not limited to low-tech positions requiring little education. Computer programmers and engineers have been replaced by workers from India, Russia, and other nations as well.

Several large-scale studies have suggested that the problem of immigrant labor is widespread, especially in areas where unemployment tends to be high to begin with. Donald Huddle of Rice University, for instance, concludes that every hundred jobs given immigrants causes the loss of twenty-five full-time jobs for native-born Americans. Huddle estimates that job loss to immigrants in 1994 alone cost U.S. taxpayers about $4 billion in government assistance to the newly unemployed; "the displaced worker himself," he adds, "loses many times this amount in wages and benefits."[43] The effect of immigrant workers on both American laborers and the American nation, according to this argument, is strongly negative.

Pro-Immigrant Sentiment

Of course, not everyone agrees with this perspective. Those who favor high immigration rates dismiss the fears and conclusions of Huddle and Steel. To begin with, those who take this position say that it is rare for an immigrant to actually displace a U.S. citizen in the job market. The reasons for this are threefold. First, as economist Julian Simon puts it, "Potential immigrants are well aware of labor-market conditions in the U.S., and they tend not to come if there is little demand for their skills."[44] The image of immigrants swarming in and pushing native-born Americans out of their jobs is much exaggerated, Simon believes. To a far greater extent, he says, immigrants take jobs only when new ones are being created for which a shortage of qualified applicants exists.

This trend is particularly true in the high-paying professions, such as engineering and medicine. "High-tech companies . . . have turned increasingly to highly skilled foreigners because of the dearth of available U.S. workers with skills needed by the firms," a journalist reports.[45] But many observers believe that the same general process holds true at other levels, citing several studies. "Immigration does not exacerbate unemployment," Simon says flatly, "even among directly competing groups."[46] If unemployment does not rise among U.S.-born workers, Simon points out, then it is hard to credit the idea that immigrants are displacing natives.

Second, the argument runs, immigrants have little effect on American workers because immigrants often fill jobs no one else wants. "I know why [immigrants] are here," said Texas governor George W. Bush in 1997. "There are a lot of jobs people in Texas won't do, [such as] laying tar in August."[47] In this view, immigrants are not competing against Americans; indeed, immigrants benefit the country by taking those jobs native-born Texans, Pennsylvanians, and Alaskans "won't do." That includes work in meatpacking plants, garment factories, and other businesses which offer employees low pay, low status, and dangerous or grueling work.

Americans Versus Immigrants

A related issue involves the perceived quality of American workers, especially those with very little education and few job skills. Some U.S. employers cite a declining work ethic among American workers. Too many arrive at their jobs late or not at all; too many put in minimal effort; too many seem unwilling or unable to learn the basic requirements of the job. To employers frustrated by the poor performance of American citizens, immigrants are the best available solution.

Immigrants work in a sweatshop. Companies often hire immigrants to work at jobs that are considered undesirable by most Americans.

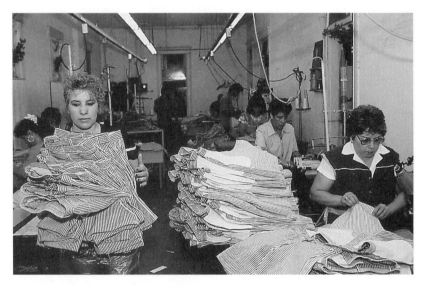

A St. Louis job placement specialist sums up the appeal of immigrant workers: "Some companies have a hard time finding people who work hard, are drug-free and are family-oriented. That's what they find here."[48]

By the same token, many immigrant workers have had a hugely positive effect on American life and the American economy. Some of the greatest inventions, scientific breakthroughs, and ideas of the last century have been the product of immigrant workers hired by American corporations. "What would [the United States] look like," wonders a businessman, "if the computer chip had been created in Europe because of our lousy immigration policy?"[49]

Job Creation

The third prong of the pro-immigration argument is perhaps the strongest. According to this perspective, immigrants do not take jobs; they create them. "Immigration benefits the American economy overall," concluded a recent report by the National Academy of Sciences.[50] By spending their earnings where they live and paying taxes, immigrants help expand the economy, thus benefiting all Americans and indirectly opening up new jobs for the native born.

Immigrants not only aid the U.S. economy by spending and paying; they also hire more workers. Immigrants own at least forty thousand companies in New York State alone, adding many thousands of jobs and billions of dollars to the state's economy. One immigration lawyer argues that immigrants tend to be extremely creative and willing to take risks that native-born entrepreneurs do not want to take. As a result, immigrants are especially likely to create successful businesses. "The rest of us ride the wave they create," he adds.[51] Far from harming American workers, this theory runs, immigrant labor actually opens up new possibilities to Americans in the job market.

Wages

Those opposed to immigrant labor dismiss these claims. Researcher Gary Burtless calls the notion that aliens only take jobs unwanted by natives "pure self-deception."[52] Donald Huddle notes that Houston construction workers receive salaries well above the median for the area. In Elgin, Illinois, a sweep by immigration officials resulted in the deportation of sixty-nine illegal aliens who held jobs. "Within hours, hundreds of local residents applied for these jobs," reports a journalist, "all of which were filled within three days."[53]

Others deny that high-tech firms truly need to seek out immigrants. Some Americans argue that the United States already turns out more doctoral students than it can provide jobs for, even in highly technical areas. Why, then, do we bring in so many professionals from other nations? Certainly these immigrants do not fill jobs that cannot be done by Americans. And if they did, some observers point out, there are other solutions: new training programs and partnerships between industries and universities, just to name two.

Likewise, opponents point out, any benefits from immigrant labor go disproportionately to certain groups of Americans, notably business owners and the rich, while leaving others behind. "The present rate of legal immigration has been a boon to employers," concedes writer Michael Lind, noting the low pay scales many of these companies offer their immigrant labor force. "And a disaster for low-income [native-born] workers."[54]

Opponents of high immigration make a second, related argument: that Americans' wages are depressed by the availability of immigrants. That is, native workers make less money than they would if there were no supply of immigrant labor. Critics of current U.S. policy cite many statistics and much anecdotal evidence suggesting that immigration tends to lower salaries. For low-wage workers especially, this leads to a double whammy. Either they lose their jobs to eager immigrants, or they take detrimental salary cuts in order to stay employed.

Again, the argument carries a certain intuitive weight. Even the lowest U.S. wages are a huge step up from the prevailing salaries in many other countries. "As inhospitable as work is at Storm Lake," says a journalist who studies the meatpacking industry, "the average wage of about $7 an hour still trumps Mexico's $4-a-day minimum."[55]

Moreover, an increase in the supply of workers means a job market in which companies have the upper hand. Employers can lower wages and still hire enough people to fill their needs. Immigration has dramatically increased the supply of workers to American companies,

A grocer waits on her customers. Opponents of immigration stress that it increases competition for low-paying, low-skill positions and reduces wages.

especially those competing for low-paying, low-skill positions. The result, again, should be a significant downward pressure on wages, with unpleasant consequences for U.S. citizens who work in these fields.

"It Is Cheap to Hire a Janitor"

Many Americans believe that there is a clear connection between immigrant labor and low wages. In some cases, they argue, wages have dropped so far that poorly skilled Americans no longer have an incentive to work; for them, welfare may actually be a better deal. "It is cheap to hire a janitor, gardener or maid," writes an observer, "so cheap that unskilled Americans are often unwilling to work at such wages. Were the going rate for orderlies and street sweepers $12 an hour rather than $4, unskilled Americans would likely fill these jobs, as natives do in Europe."[56] In this view, U.S. citizens are being priced completely out of the labor market by such reliance on cheap immigrant workers.

Several studies tend to support this perspective. The salaries of the lowest-paid workers in the United States have indeed been dropping. And the changes are most noticeable in occupations that are increasingly populated by immigrants. In Los Angeles, for example, maintenance salaries dropped 40 percent as native-born Americans were being replaced by Hispanic immigrants. Economist George Borjas estimates that native-born workers lose an aggregate $114 billion a year as the result of wage depression caused by immigrant labor. Likewise, two University of Houston researchers found a noticeable trend in wages among southwestern municipalities. In general, the lower the immigrant population in a town, the higher the salaries.

An immigrant from El Salvador does landscaping work. Some studies show that the salaries of the lowest-paid workers drop in areas densely populated with immigrants.

Alternative Explanations

Proponents of immigration generally concede that wage depression can happen, especially in certain industries and in communities where the immigrant population is high. Still, they argue, any monetary loss is negligible. While the University of Houston study did find a correlation between immigrant population density and salaries, one writer points out that most of the difference in earnings was accounted for by differences in the costs of living. "There may be some downward pressure on wages," concludes a researcher, "but it's very difficult to see it at a local level." [57]

Similarly, immigration may not be solely to blame for the economic dislocations of the last few decades. Most scholars accept that the gap between rich and poor is growing, but many are unwilling to attribute much of the spread to immigrants. Tax laws, increasing globalization, education gaps—all are implicated. Indeed, several studies suggest that immigration, far from hurting wages, actually has the opposite effect. One, for instance, found that African Americans earned higher salaries if they lived in cities with high immigrant populations.

And in any case, some argue, a lowering of wages is not necessarily a bad thing. From a strictly economic perspective, wages are supposed to be subject to fluctuation in a capitalist society. That helps keep both business and workers flexible, and leads in the end to a more balanced and productive economy. Moreover, all Americans benefit from lower costs of goods and services when U.S. businesses hire poorly paid immigrant workers. "People still want to buy lettuce at 30 cents a head," explains an immigration advocate. "They can only do that because the people who pick it are working for such low wages." [58] This fact may not excuse the damage done to any American workers who lose their jobs to immigrants, but it does lessen the effect on the country as a whole.

Unresolved Debate

The issue of immigrants and jobs may never come to a resolution. The rhetoric on both sides can be strident and the tone impatient; each camp has its collective mind made up. On the one hand, the

Migrant farmworkers harvest and box lettuce.

Wall Street Journal proposes a pro-immigrant constitutional amendment that reads "There shall be open borders,"[59] and a journalist states flatly that "the U.S. shouldn't bar entry to creative and skilled people at all."[60] On the other, a politician asks, "These people need jobs, but where will they find them? Are you willing to give them yours?"[61]

That the issue is passionately debated is understandable: The availability of work and the right to work are fundamental concerns. If immigration has the effect of costing Americans their jobs and lowering Americans' wages, then it is difficult to see why the government should support it. On the other hand, if immigration expands the economy and increases Americans' wealth, then the government ought to make attracting immigrants a priority.

Of course, jobs are not the only question. Immigration may help the economy and still be undesirable for other reasons; it may even take away some jobs and have an overall positive effect based on other factors. Moreover, the truth of the jobs question may lie somewhere in between: perhaps immigration hurts *some* American workers while helping *many*, or vice versa. But more than other aspects of the immigration debate, the jobs issue affects all Americans in an obvious and immediate way: in their pocketbooks. American wealth—and by extension, Americans' futures—depends on the way the U.S. government chooses to resolve this question.

Should Immigrants Be Denied Access to Government Services?

IN NOVEMBER 1994, the state of California adopted Proposition 187. The measure, approved by a comfortable majority of voters in a statewide election, made it impossible for California's large population of illegal aliens to receive various benefits from the state. According to 187, for instance, illegals were not permitted to collect welfare benefits or food stamps, and much of the publicly funded Medi-Cal medical benefits system was likewise placed off limits. In addition, the law banned the children of illegal aliens from attending the state's public schools.

To many Californians, the law simply made sense. Supporters of the proposition produced statistics suggesting that California's limited social services budgets were being stretched past the breaking point by illegal immigrants, who after all were in the state only by violating immigration law. They also claimed that large numbers of aliens were attracted to California precisely because of the generous benefits package the state offered. Cut back on the aid, so the reasoning went, and the torrent of illegal migrants would become a trickle.

By keeping unwanted, undocumented aliens out and by reserving scarce resources for truly needy American citizens, proponents argued, America would be better off if Californians took a stand. The best interest of Americans, or at the very least Californians, lay in limiting most social services to U.S. citizens and legal immigrants.

An Issue for the Courts

But the law provoked immediate controversy. Despite the overall ease of its passage, many Californians vehemently opposed the measure. In part, the argument against the proposition focused on its effect on immigrants themselves. Certainly the law had the potential to harm illegal aliens who relied on the schools to teach their children, welfare benefits to make ends meet on low wages, and inexpensive medical care for sudden illnesses or injuries. Many opponents called Proposition 187 barbaric and cruel; some charged that people would die as a result of it.

Other opponents argued that the measure, despite all appearances, was not in the best interest of American citizens. They believed that the average illegal alien was attracted to California not by the promise of a handout, but rather by the hope of a job; therefore, the proposition would do little or nothing to curb the problem of illegal immigration. They challenged pro-187 statistics about the effect of illegals on social service organizations, citing instead figures that suggested that illegal aliens as a group paid more into the system via taxes than

Advocates and opponents of California Proposition 187, a law prohibiting illegal aliens from receiving various state benefits, confront one another during a demonstration.

they took out in benefits. Finally, they claimed that California was better off if all residents—immigrant and native alike—were healthy, educated, and well fed rather than sick, ignorant, and hungry.

Proposition 187 never went into effect. Challenged in court almost as soon as it was passed, its provisions were set aside while it was subjected to judicial scrutiny. In 1997, when a federal judge ruled that the law violated the Constitution, the measure died. Opponents were delighted, calling the decision a victory not only for illegal immigrants but also for Americans as a whole. Supporters of 187 were predictably dismayed; they termed the decision a mistake that would ultimately harm the country.

For now, the debate over Proposition 187 is over. None of its major provisions are a part of California law today; indeed, for the most part, illegal immigrants to California today receive the same benefits for which they were eligible before passage of 187. But the larger debate over public benefits for illegal immigrants continues. Many states have similar provisions in place, upheld by judges, which restrict the types of benefits that illegal aliens can receive. Indeed, while most of these laws have been directed specifically at illegal immigrants, the debate has recently expanded to include legal immigrants as well. The federal government itself has limited the ability of legal immigrants to collect certain welfare payments. Though 187 may not be in place, its example has influenced many other laws. Its place as groundbreaking legislation is assured.

The Costs of Immigration

It is undeniable that large chunks of some government budgets are given over to immigrants, legal and otherwise. The two most obvious examples are schools and medical care. "Immigrants come in," says a researcher. "They have kids. The kids use our schools, they use our medical system, and that's expensive."[62] According to one recent estimate, for instance, the families of nine hundred thousand California schoolchildren are here illegally. The total cost of educating them—paid directly from the pockets of California state and local taxpayers—amounts to between $3.5 and $6 billion a year.

Medical services, too, are heavily used by immigrants. In 1994, the cost of providing emergency medical care to illegal aliens was

In California, educating immigrants costs between $3.5 and $6 billion a year.

estimated at $7.5 billion. Nor are illegals the only immigrants who use public money. "In California," writes commentator Dan Stein, "23.7% of newly naturalized citizens are receiving Medicaid benefits, compared with 8.2% of Californians as a whole."[63]

Other forms of welfare payments are going disproportionately to immigrants as well. The 1990 census revealed that most government programs, such as Aid to Families with Dependent Children and public housing assistance, were used by a higher percentage of immigrant households than ones headed by native-born Americans. Food stamps, for example, were issued to 6.5 percent of native households but 9.2 percent of immigrant households.

To be sure, these statistics do not tell the whole story. Social Security and Medicare, for example, are not much used by immigrants. Taking them into consideration changes the situation dramatically. "When programs for the elderly are included," writes Julian Simon, "immigrant families receive far *less* in public services than natives."[64] Similarly, most comparisons leave out the government money contributed by working immigrants in taxes and Social Security withholdings. Adding in these payments also brings the level of contribution closer to the level of benefits for immigrants.

Expenses

Nevertheless, many Americans worry about the cost of providing services to immigrants, particularly those here illegally. Not only is the expense large, to many Americans it also seems misplaced. Every dollar paid out in educating the child of an illegal alien, for example, is a dollar that could instead go to the general welfare of the schools. Former California governor Pete Wilson has pointed out that the costs of educating illegal aliens, if applied to citizens and legal immigrants only, would enable his state to add tutoring services for high school students, expand preschool and day care offerings, and purchase new and powerful computers for classrooms.

Financial considerations aside, some observers are also troubled by the ethics of policies that grant eligibility for services to illegal immigrants. Those who are not here legally, these people argue, should not be entitled to the same benefits as those who were born here or arrived through proper channels. "Illegals in need of medical services should return to their native lands," a legal scholar says in support of more restrictive measures.[65] Some people go further, suggesting that benefits be denied to all noncitizens. In this view, Americans' primary responsibility ought to be to those who were born U.S. citizens or who have formally declared loyalty to the United States, not to those who have yet to make a commitment to a new country.

"Welcome to America!"

Many of those who wish to reduce immigrant eligibility for benefits also believe that generous welfare payments are entirely too attractive to immigrants. Instead of coming to America in search of good jobs, upward mobility, and a better life through hard work, so this argument runs, immigrants arrive in hopes of collecting welfare. "Welcome to America!" former North Carolina senator Lauch Faircloth said sarcastically during a congressional debate on immigrant aid. "You *know* when you leave where you are, you'll be eligible for food stamps, and you won't *ever* have to work, 'cause we'll feed you!"[66]

Indeed, there is evidence that benefits are a pull for some immigrants. Bookstores in Hong Kong and Taiwan, reports one observer, "sell a Chinese-language book that contains a 36-page guide to SSI

A frequent complaint lodged by immigration opponents is the apparent high cost of providing government services to illegal immigrants.

[Supplemental Security Income] and other benefits."[67] The attraction of free prenatal care encourages many women to come to California, some charge. "They only know how to say two things in English," one hospital worker complains. "They want a birth certificate [for the child] and they want to know how to apply for the WIC [Women, Infants and Children] program."[68]

Moreover, generous welfare benefits may encourage people to stay even if the United States is not truly right for them. Several generations ago, many immigrants used to return to their homelands after a few years in the United States. Today, however, immigrants are much more likely to stay. The difference, some believe, is the availability of welfare. But the United States is probably not helped by having immigrants who are motivated by a desire for "free" money. "It is suicidal," says Senator Phil Gramm, "for a nation to set up procedures to attract people to come to this country not with a dream of achievement, but with a dream of living off the fruits of someone else's labor." [69]

Legislative Reform

Concerns such as these have led to many attempts to limit or slash immigrant eligibility for various benefits. Proposition 187 is merely one of the most visible. More sweeping legislation was the federal welfare reform bill of 1996. That measure cut off nearly all kinds of federal payments to immigrants, legal and illegal alike, including Medicaid, SSI, food stamps, and much more. The welfare reform bill shifted many of the burdens of these payments, via block grants, to the states, which could decide for themselves whether or not to offer them to immigrants. Many immediately declared that they would not do so.

But like Proposition 187, the welfare reform bill has proved to be less than the final word on the subject. Many of the cuts mandated by the bill have since been restored on the federal level. And while most states opted not to make up the missing benefits, some opted to do exactly that. In all, seventeen states chose to continue providing food stamps, for example, after federal food aid was cut off to legal immigrants. California, the most popular destination for immigrants, has continued to offer most services no longer provided by the national government.

In fact, there is a strong counterargument to the notion that aliens should not be receiving benefits. Besides worrying about the harm done to immigrants themselves, many opponents of reductions believe that denying benefits to immigrants is simply bad policy. Eliminating immigrants from schools, welfare rolls, the Social Security system, and all but emergency medical care has consequences for all Americans. Immigrant children who are not permitted to attend school, for instance, will grow up to be ignorant and unskilled. Many experts see this mixture as a recipe for disaster. Disaffected teenagers may see drugs and crime as their only future; potentially they present serious problems for the towns in which they live. "In a state [California] that is already struggling to educate its children properly and fight crime in the streets," warns an editorialist, "it is hardly good policy to throw a couple of hundred thousand children out of school." [70]

An elderly Chinese immigrant participates in a demonstration against immigration legislation passed by Congress in 1996.

The same social costs hold true with medicine. It may well be in Americans' self-interest to provide medical care to immigrants, since even one alien carrying a communicable, untreated disease such as tuberculosis can put an entire local population at risk. "When all low-income residents receive prenatal care," writes one California advocate, "lives are saved, communicable diseases are screened, and Medi-Cal costs are greatly reduced."[71] Indeed, providing benefits may actually save money in the long run. By one reckoning, California would save $9 million annually as a result of excluding illegal immigrants from its health plan—but pay $47 million more in emergency treatment for the same illegals and extra public health costs for citizens.

Cutting Illegal Immigration?

Furthermore, many pro-immigration advocates reject the notion that immigrants arrive strictly to collect services. "There is no evidence that Hispanic immigrants—legal or illegal—come to the United States looking for a handout," says columnist Linda Chavez.[72] In fact, most immigrants are employed. That some receive welfare payments simply indicates the low wages immigrants often receive; poor salaries, not the immigration laws, are the culprit, from this perspective.

If immigrants come to the United States primarily for jobs, then of course part of the antibenefit argument is weakened. Another important conclusion is that rolling back benefits will not affect immigration rates. A handful of prospective immigrants, attracted today by easily available benefits, would decide not to come after all. Similarly, those disenchanted by the new lack of services would return home. But the large majority of immigrants would not be deterred by the lack of benefits. As they typically do now, they would arrive to work. There would be no significant reduction in immigration levels, no mass return of immigrants to their homelands. Cutting benefits would serve only to make life more difficult for the neediest of these immigrants.

Areas of Agreement

Despite differences of opinion, there are areas of agreement between those in favor of extending benefits to immigrants and those in favor of cutting them. Nearly all observers believe that certain states and cities are suffering unduly from the burden of providing immigrant services, notably health care and schools. Certainly the expense of educating children of undocumented workers is far higher in Texas or California than it is in Maine or Utah, for example. And Florida or Illinois have to pay a good deal more in immigrant services than do states which attract relatively few immigrants.

These numbers are not merely theoretical. One study determined that immigration has little immediate effect on the finances of native households. "The costs to native-born workers are small, and so are the benefits," sums up an economist who helped conduct

An immigrant boy expresses his intent to remain in America during a Latino march in Washington, D.C.

the research.[73] The study went on to add, however, that native-born Californians face a startlingly different situation. The immigrant levels in that state require its citizens to pay much more than most other states. "The average [California] household," says a reporter, "pays an extra $1,178 in taxes because of immigrants."[74] Thinkers on both sides agree that something is wrong here. One proposal is to provide extra federal assistance to those local and state governments seriously affected by needy immigrants.

Steps Toward Agreement

There has been movement toward compromise in recent years. Even some staunch pro-immigrant voices have admitted that abuses of the welfare system have been entirely too common, and that immigrants should perhaps not expect a full range of services from the United States—at least, not right away. The welfare reform bill contained a clause that required would-be immigrants to show that they would not become public charges dependent on welfare payments. The *Los Angeles Times* editorialized against the bill as a whole, but added that the public charge section was a "necessary [and] reasonable requirement." [75]

Likewise, few commentators write from as strong a pro-immigrant perspective as columnist Linda Chavez, but even Chavez has seen some good in the welfare reform bill. "If the harsh rhetoric of the 1990s encouraged many immigrants who were receiving benefits to leave the welfare rolls," she writes, "it could turn out to be a huge blessing in disguise—not just for taxpayers, but for the immigrants themselves." [76] In her view, the availability of welfare has encouraged some immigrants to rely on social services rather than working hard. To this extent, cracking down on eligibility has only helped improve productivity and overall quality of life.

In the opposing camp, antibenefit commentators increasingly seem to accept the need for some benefits. This is especially true where longtime legal immigrants are concerned. Cutting the disability, retirement, and health benefits of these "almost Americans" strikes many U.S. citizens as poor policy at best and mean-spirited at worst. "When it came to throwing somebody's grandmother out on the street," says an observer, explaining why some proposals to limit services for legal immigrants have failed, "no one wanted to do that." [77] Even George Borjas, one of the leading voices arguing that immigrants use more than their fair share of services, draws a distinction between cutting off present-day immigrants and denying the same benefits to future newcomers.

Similarly, the year after the welfare reform bill passed, many of those who had eagerly voted for cuts in immigrant services turned around and restored a few of the more controversial benefits, notably Medicaid and supplemental security payments to nearly half a million legal immigrants. "All these compromises we made . . . were fine," says a Senate Republican aide. "They did not violate the heart of our bill."[78] Most opponents recognize that some immigrant services are helpful to immigrants themselves, and to the country as well.

It is unlikely that the two sides in this controversy will entirely agree. There will always be differences of opinion about the validity of statistical evidence; there will be an even more significant disparity in the way people choose to interpret the evidence. Still, modest compromises augur well for the future. Chavez, Borjas, and others are looking at the question of providing benefits to immigrants through a careful examination of the facts, rather than falling back on sweeping political rhetoric to make snap decisions. The question of immigrants and services has important implications for the future of the nation. The more we can look at this issue in a dispassionate, nonpartisan way, the better will be our chances of making wise and ethical choices.

Chapter 4

Should Efforts to Halt Illegal Immigration Be Strengthened?

LOCATED SOUTHEAST OF TUCSON, practically astride the Mexican border, the town of Douglas, Arizona, is home to about seventeen thousand people, most of them Hispanic Americans. For many years, Douglas was a quiet and relatively peaceful place. Its proximity to Mexico did distinguish it from similar cities in other parts of the country, however. Once in a while a resident of Mexico or some other nation, denied permission to legally immigrate to the United States, would try to slip across the border near Douglas to become one of the many undocumented workers living in the United States.

Still, Douglas was far from a popular crossing. Surrounded mainly by desert, it was not close to any major population centers. Nor was it large enough to provide many jobs to those who wished to take advantage of relatively high salaries in the United States. Most people attempting illegal entry tried to cross the border closer to their own homes and into large cities. Together, the sections of the border near El Paso, Texas, and San Diego, California, attracted about two-thirds of those who wanted to get across illegally. The few who came across near Douglas were exceptions, and they had little impact on Douglas itself.

But in 1993, that situation began to change. The U.S. Border Patrol, an arm of the Immigration and Naturalization Service (INS), stepped up enforcement operations in El Paso and San Diego. The patrol added officers, purchased new equipment, and increased

Workers erect a fence in El Paso, Texas, along the Mexican border. Prior to 1993, two-thirds of all illegal border crossings occurred near El Paso and San Diego, California.

penalties for illegal immigrants. In one sense the operation was a major success. Many fewer illegal immigrants successfully crossed the border near those two cities. The San Diego and El Paso crossings had been tightened significantly.

However, the operations had only a local impact. People intent on reaching the United States simply found a new place to cross the border. For many undocumented workers, that place was Douglas. In 1993, the first year of the new programs, the Border Patrol caught twenty-seven thousand people trying to cross near Douglas. Every year since then, the numbers have gone up, soaring to levels unimaginable only a short time ago. In March 1999 alone, another twenty-seven thousand migrants were detained. Over just six years, the annual total had become the monthly total.

"We're Being Invaded"

The illegal immigrants have created significant problems for Douglas and the surrounding area. "We're being invaded," says Douglas's mayor.[79] In their haste to cross to safety, illegals trespass on residents' cattle ranges and yards. Dumping of garbage has been a serious problem. Aliens simply drop water bottles, extra clothes, and other supplies wherever they need to, especially if patrol officers are on their trail. "Residents are disgusted and concerned by the debris trespassers leave behind," writes a reporter, mentioning "piles of excrement, soiled diapers . . . plastic jugs and drug syringes." [80]

Worse, the illegals frequently damage property or even break into houses. Sometimes the damage is done out of ignorance. "I lost two cows and two calves in the last year after they ingested plastic" dropped by migrants, says a rancher. [81] Sometimes it has been done out of desperate need. Water-tank valves have been wrenched open, water pipes cut by immigrants whose own water supplies ran low. "When you're in a serious drought," says a rancher, "as we have been, [cutting pipes and opening valves] could be a catastrophe." [82] One woman says her house has been burglarized twenty-five times; at least some burglars were hungry invaders looking only for food.

But some of the damage is deliberate and has citizens of Douglas worried. "I've been burglarized, had a truck stolen and property vandalized," says rancher Larry Vance. "There's no privacy anymore, no peace and quiet. There's thousands of people running through this valley every night." [83] Many citizens have taken to carrying guns and setting up expensive surveillance equipment. Others have bought dogs. No resident has been harmed to date, but many believe the day is not far off.

Enforcement of Border Controls

The Border Patrol has stepped up enforcement of border controls in the last few years. Many more officers now roam the area than did a few years ago. But "many more" is still far from enough when thousands try to cross every single day. The border near Douglas runs through rugged territory; it would be difficult to seal even if the patrol had twice its current level of manpower. And with Mexicans, Central Americans, and other aliens desperate to enter the United States at almost any cost, the task of keeping illegals out is much, much harder.

The situation in Douglas illustrates one of the most complex debates regarding American immigration: the pros and cons of trying to keep undocumented aliens out of the country. The government's inability to seal the border, say some residents, has had a terrible effect on their lives; therefore, according to this argument, the government is obligated to do much more than it has to ensure the safety and comfort of its citizens.

Other observers, however, draw a very different moral from Douglas's experience—that illegal immigration cannot truly be controlled. Closing the borders in El Paso and San Diego simply encouraged migrants to cross at Douglas instead; thus, sealing the border at Douglas would probably only force illegals to detour to crossings even more remote. Poor and desperate for work, many aliens will take great risks to reach the United States safely. Virtually no amount of money or show of force will stop illegal immigration, and any attempts to do so are doomed to failure.

Statistical Profile

Any noncitizen who enters the country without the official permission of the Immigration and Naturalization Service has arrived in the United States illegally. Not all of these illegals are truly immigrants. Many intend to go back to their home countries in a year or two; some from Mexico cross the border regularly for daily work, and a few function almost as commuters who live in one nation and work in another. But a large proportion of illegals consists of people who do intend to settle permanently in the United States. In any case, the terms "illegal alien," "illegal immigrant," and "undocumented worker" are all used more or less interchangeably.

Illegal aliens arrive from all over the world. Increasing numbers of illegal aliens arrive from China, Central America, and Eastern Europe, for example, as well as Mexico. Some scale fences, ford rivers, and scurry through deserts along the national border with Mexico. Others arrive by water. In one several-month stretch during the early 1990s, immigration officials intercepted twenty-four ships carrying illegal aliens from China; it is assumed that many more successfully made it to shore. Still others arrive by air. Many illegals enter quite legally on student or tourist visas, then simply fail to leave when their official time runs out.

Nobody knows how many illegal immigrants live in the United States. Illegal immigration is a shadowy affair. Undocumented

Two illegal immigrants pry open a fence in order to cross into the United States.

workers do not reveal themselves to census takers or brag about their status. As a result, researchers can do little more than guess at numbers, and the guesses vary considerably. Recent estimates have ranged from 2 million illegals in the United States all the way up to 12 million. The most careful research suggests between 3 and 6 million, but even these studies are open to serious question. As a government office put it, "There is simply no statistically reliable measurement of the undocumented alien population."[84]

Most illegals are workers who serve in low-paying jobs. Sweatshops in New York City, restaurants in Chicago, and assembly lines in Houston all hire illegals. Planters in California's Central Valley rely on undocumented aliens to pick their apples, oranges, and asparagus. Illegals are an increasing presence in many of America's smaller towns and cities, too, even those far from national borders. "Almost everywhere in America," writes a journalist, illegal workers "make beds, change diapers and mow lawns."[85] A few illegals are well-educated professionals, especially from Asia or Europe, but the bulk of the undocumented are poorly educated, poorly skilled, and poorly paid.

National Security

The argument over illegal aliens has an unusually broad range. In part, illegal immigration is controversial precisely because it is illegal. Concerned though Americans may be about the effect of legal immigrants on jobs and benefits, legal immigrants are here because of a national consensus that they are valuable and wanted. Illegal immigrants, on the other hand, are here despite a consensus that they are *not* wanted. While some Americans argue that illegals are especially likely to take on jobs that natives do not want, most find it hard to justify giving benefits or employment to illegals while natives are not getting what they need.

A second issue regarding aliens is one of fairness. The American government has set up rules and policies regarding immigration, and has asked would-be immigrants to respect and obey them. Many legal immigrants have done exactly that, waiting to leave home until their turn arrived. Some are still waiting. Illegal immigrants, in contrast, are ignoring the rules and jumping to the front of the line. Many Americans find this kind of behavior unfair and ethically questionable—another reason to crack down on illegal immigration.

But perhaps the most critical issue surrounding illegal immigrants today is the security of the nation's borders. As the case of Douglas indicates, the national boundaries are far from closed; a determined alien can find ways of getting across the line. Moreover, illegals often have little or no trouble staying in the United States after arriving. "You're not going to get deported unless you've gotten into a whole lot of trouble," says an immigration lawyer.[86]

The Border Patrol

That U.S. borders are porous is hard to deny. "The first duty of a sovereign nation is to control its borders," says former senator Alan Simpson. "We do not."[87] The INS itself admits that two or three illegals cross the line for every one who is apprehended. Some place the number far higher. Groups that take money from would-be aliens and smuggle them across the U.S. border "operate with near impunity," concludes a U.S. intelligence report.[88] While not all immigrants have such an easy time crossing the border, enough do to lend credence to Simpson's complaint.

The ease of entry is caused by several factors. First, the Border Patrol is seriously understaffed. The El Paso station is in charge of eighty-five thousand square miles of territory, mostly mountain and

Immigration protesters try to rally support for the U.S. Border Patrol. Understaffed and lacking resources, the Border Patrol is unable to effectively curtail illegal immigration.

desert, but has fewer patrol officers than a typical big city police department. Budgets for the Border Patrol are historically small and notoriously vulnerable to congressional cuts. Thus, equipment is often outdated or broken. "The dilapidated vehicles [used by the Border Patrol at Imperial Beach, California] are known to break down during chases," writes reporter Sebastian Rotella. "More than half the fleet is unusable."[89]

The lack of resources has other implications as well. Many illegals carry papers—temporary resident cards, birth certificates, Social Security documents, and the like—that would appear to justify their entry. Most of these documents, however, are counterfeit. Good scanning equipment, extra training, or more time to scrutinize each piece of identification would go a long way toward preventing these aliens from entering the country. Low funding, however, dooms the effort.

Other Causes

Another reason for high illegal immigration is the light penalty given aliens who try to cross. Virtually all undocumented workers caught crossing the border in the Southwest are simply returned to the other side. Those who are not—less than 1 percent of the total— are typically detained for a few days, a week or two at the most, before being deported. This treatment discourages few illegals from trying again—and again and again and again, in some cases. Even a two-week detention, a reporter writes, is "a small price to pay for access to life in the United States."[90] The lack of significant punishment not only encourages illegals to try their luck at crossing the border; it has an effect on U.S. officials, too. "The feeling is that all they're doing is spitting into the ocean, accomplishing nothing," says a recently retired border agent. "Morale has bottomed out."[91]

A third problem is the enormous number of possible entry points into the country. Few fences or natural boundaries separate the United States from its neighbors. The six thousand miles of border the United States shares with Canada and Mexico, together with the number of seaports and international airports, make this a very hard country to patrol effectively, especially a nation that prides itself on an open and free-flowing society.

A fourth reason is the attraction of life in the United States. Even a wage of $5.50 an hour may look good to one used to laboring all day for less than that. Some Chinese illegals call the United States "the beautiful country." [92] "Once we're here," agrees a man from Ecuador, "we'll do anything to stay." [93] Many who try to settle permanently in the United States are fleeing economic hardships; others are running from political repression or social chaos. Others hope to work their way to wealth in a new society, or want the benefits of a more open culture. To be sure, some illegals do not choose

Many illegal immigrants come to the United States in order to escape from economic hardship.

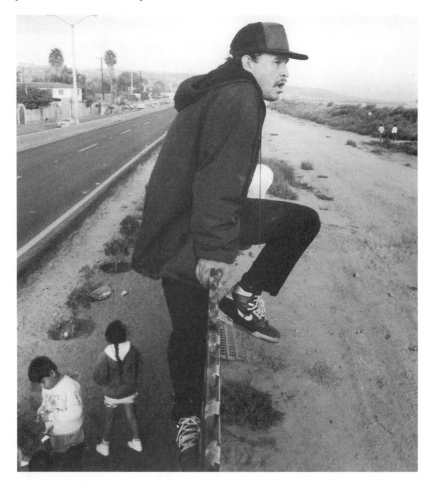

to stay, but for many, America is a haven—a refuge worth a great deal of trouble to reach.

Ultimately, the answer to the problem of illegal immigration lies in the nations from which the immigrants come. As long as financial policies consign a large share of a country's population to desperate poverty, people will try to make a life in a land where people are better off. Most experts agree that the United States should extend more economic help to nations that are home to many would-be illegal immigrants. While other people advocate a slightly different range of actions on the part of the United States, most see some kind of help as critical to eliminating illegal immigration.

A Show of Force

But such a solution lies in the long term. In the near term, many Americans have offered quick solutions to the problem of easy entry. Some of these answers involve beefing up the Border Patrol. Certainly experience, as well as common sense, suggests that more agents make for a safer border. "It's getting tougher," said a Mexican citizen about the San Diego crossing after the 1993 crackdown went into effect. "I used to cross almost every weekend. . . . Now they have more agents."[94] California representative Elton Gallegly suggests doubling the number of agents, and many officials agree: With a sufficient show of force, illegal immigration can be curbed.

Other observers point out that new technology would go a long way toward solving the problem. Surveillance cameras, helicopters, and infrared telescopes could all aid INS agents charged with cutting off illegal traffic into this country. Some call for both expanded technology and expanded manpower. "The federal government must secure our border," says Pete Wilson. "They must devote the manpower and the technology necessary to prevent people from crossing the border in the first place."[95]

Another frequently heard suggestion is to erect physical barriers along the borders. Political commentator and candidate Patrick Buchanan has called for the construction of high fences, walls, and ditches all along the Mexican border. A steel fence near San Diego has helped reduce illegal border crossings. California politician Duncan Hunter urges the construction of a three-layer fence along the border. To save money, some suggest that fences and walls be erected only across the most populated parts of the border, since the more remote areas are already hard to cross.

And a few Americans, especially those who live in areas of highest traffic, have a more dramatic idea: Militarize the border. California senator Barbara Boxer has called for National Guard help in patrolling her

Political commentator and presidential candidate Pat Buchanan has called for high fences, walls, and ditches to be constructed along the Mexican border.

state's southern boundary. Others urge the intervention of the U.S. Army itself. "We need the military," says Douglas mayor Larry Vance.[96] The armed forces have helped the Border Patrol in some capacities in the past, and some believe that their role should be increased.

Not all suggestions involve patrols or barriers, though. Stiffening penalties for those caught trying to cross might help limit illegal immigration, some Americans argue. This need not mean jailing migrants. Mexicans, for instance, says a former INS head, should be sent back to the interior of their country when captured rather than dumped just across the border. Streamlining the process might be effective as well. Aliens who arrive by air, for instance, could have their cases heard the day their planes land. An alien who cannot present valid documentation could be shipped home on the next available flight.

Doomed to Failure

Most of these measures, however, do not have overwhelming support among Americans. Not everyone sees illegal immigration as a huge threat to the American way of life. Others worry about the cost of trying to fence off even a small part of the border with Mexico, or the expense of doubling the number of border agents. Still others fret that the notion of barriers is antithetical to America's claim to be a true democracy. "Walls send the wrong signal from a nation that proclaims to be a free society," says an opponent of physical barriers.[97]

The costs associated with changes would indeed be large. Even if not all sections of the Mexican border are fenced off, the proposed fences are high, strong, and expensive. Suggested changes in detention practices require money, too. At present the INS can hold only about seven of every one hundred illegals who arrive at John F. Kennedy Airport in New York City. The rest are released on condition that they come back for a hearing at a later date. Not surprisingly, most never reappear. It will take a major infusion of cash to provide facilities that will change these statistics.

Moreover, some Americans believe that more fences and agents will have little effect. For many illegals, migration to the United States means the difference between having a decent life and no hope at all. "In Mexico we don't have work," says an illegal alien. "They

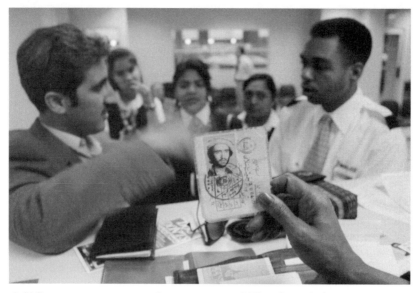

A U.S. customs agent questions a suspected illegal immigrant at an airport.

can put an agent every meter, but they won't stop [immigration]."[98] Many others, aliens and Americans alike, echo this perspective.

Besides, as the situation in Douglas suggests, if a border is tightened at one end, it may well weaken at the other. The same scenario has occurred in airports, too; when Los Angeles's airports cracked down on illegal travelers, the problem in New York's airports worsened. In fact, it may be that trying to close off entry points creates more problems than it solves. Some studies indicate higher rates of injury and death among illegals who have tried to cross the border since the building of barriers. Making entry into the United States more difficult may create other problems, too. "The buildup [in San Diego] pushed more immigrants into the hands of smuggling mafias" who take money in exchange for help in bringing immigrants across borders illegally, points out Sebastian Rotella.[99] In this view, the barriers have not stopped or even slowed illegal immigration; they have, however, helped bring organized crime into an already complex and controversial situation.

The prospect of more INS or military support along the borders also does not sit well with all Americans. Some cite incompetence, brutality, and corruption within the Border Patrol. They worry that such abuses will continue, no matter how much budgets may be increased and how many administrators are replaced. The military, too, has been criticized for its actions along the border. In 1997, for instance, a marine on patrol mistakenly shot and killed a Mexican high school student who was tending his goats close to the Texas-Mexico border. Adding more officers may only increase tensions.

The possibility of more serious punishment raises issues of its own. The American system of justice requires fair hearings for all accused criminals, which in turn requires time and resources. Where will the illegals be housed while awaiting trial? At what cost, and at whose expense? Trials cost money. So do prisons or other detention centers. Besides that, jails are already overcrowded in many parts of the country. Opponents of stiffer penalties argue that there is little reason to lock people up simply because they are trying to get a better life. The costs of doing so are simply too high.

Already Here

The problem of identifying the several million illegal aliens who are already here is perhaps even trickier. The low profile they keep, combined with Americans' emphasis on privacy rights, can make it hard to tell them from legal immigrants—sometimes even native citizens—without intense investigation. But any real attempt to protect this nation's borders must make the effort to find and deport those who are here illegally.

Many advocates of deportation believe that the problem is more a matter of will than a truly intractable puzzle. If the United States decided to treat illegals strictly as criminals, these people assert, then it could easily make life uncomfortable for many of those who have made their homes here. Among these measures are stiffer penalties for illegals caught in the country, swifter application of the existing laws, and more money given over to enforcement—suggestions familiar in other aspects of immigration.

All immigrants are supposed to provide documents to their employers that prove they are here legally; technically, employers are not supposed to hire those who lack such documentation. But in practice many do, despite the threat of jail time and fines of up to

An illegal immigrant disembarks from a Department of Justice bus. Because they keep a low profile, illegal immigrants already in the United States are difficult to identify.

$3,000. "Got this call from some guy who openly admitted on the telephone that he didn't have papers," remembers a small business owner. "Sounded surprised when I told him I wasn't interested. Acted like everybody did it."[100]

Some observers suggest that more forceful penalties be imposed on employers who knowingly hire illegal aliens. In theory at least, these should be effective; employer sanctions have often been called the key to eliminating illegal immigration. A fine of $15,000 or even $30,000 per illegal alien would go a long way toward convincing employers not to hire them at all. One surprise inspection would more than wipe out any cost savings from hiring illegal workers. Likewise, employers who took the prospect of a jail term seriously would be much more likely to demand verification of immigration status from prospective workers.

Identification

A single national database would go a long way toward informing employers—and government agencies—which job applicants are legally in the country and which are not. Some progress has been made toward this goal. Already the INS and Social Security registries are in the process of merging.

Such a program would necessarily require some sort of identity card—a means of proving that the person applying for a job is the same person listed in the database. Exactly what form this card might take is open to question. The card would have to be difficult, if not impossible, to counterfeit; thus, it would need to carry information highly specific to its holder. That might mean a Social Security–type number, or it could mean more. Alan Simpson describes a "slide-through card like you use with a Visa when you make a purchase [with] perhaps some type of driver's license photograph [or] retina examination."[101] Other advocates would encode cards with fingerprints or voice patterns. The more closely the card is linked to its holder, the less open to fraud the program will be. Therefore, supporters say, the card will cut down illegal immigration.

Cost, Privacy, and Will

These suggestions, however, are no more popular than those offered in defense of closing the border. While many Americans support them, others object on economic and ethical grounds. The issue of cost is of particular concern. The expense of patrolling airports, seaports, and land borders is slight compared with the expense of seeking out illegals across fifty states. Enforcement of existing laws is often minimal. In one three-year period, for example, only 2 percent of U.S. employers had been visited by an INS agent to make sure employees were legally entitled to be in the country. To make the threat of employer sanctions stick, budgets would have to be increased several times over.

The specter of a national database and an identity card also worries many Americans. Early returns on trial programs have not been impressive. Merged databases leave people out, invent inaccurate information, and confuse pieces of data. Moreover, the notion reminds some of a totalitarian government. Citizens in a democracy with a strong tradition of individual rights and privacy should not have to carry around cards to prove who they are, many observers argue. "The promise of a national identification system is that it would make government more efficient and effective," says a journalist. "That's also the problem." [102]

A more "efficient and effective" government could keep careful tabs on its citizens, perhaps interfering with their right to privacy. Some Americans believe that the possibility of a police state is more of a threat to America than the presence of illegal aliens could ever be. Certain businesses—notably restaurants, garment factories, and produce farms—rely heavily on illegal workers and might even collapse without illegal alien labor. For this reason, a few observers believe that attempts to impose employer sanctions are doomed. Indeed, in this view it would be foolish to exclude illegal immigrants. "The day they kick out the Mexicans," a reporter writes, summing up the argument, "is the day that the United States falls apart." [103]

There are social costs associated with a crackdown on illegals, too. In the wake of Proposition 187, California teacher Laura Simon

Farmworkers labor in an asparagus field. Many produce farms rely heavily on the work of illegal immigrants.

was asked by one of her students, an illegal alien, if Simon "was now a cop who would kick her out of school." [104] Many Americans believe that teachers, doctors, and others who serve aliens should not be involved in blowing the whistle on illegals. The need for trust is too important where education and health are concerned. Yet a serious attempt to deport undocumented workers would have to include those who teach and treat them.

"Modest Results"

Few Americans support illegal immigration as a policy. Yet Americans are nevertheless divided on the question of how hard the government should try to stop illegals. Some insist that the goal is so important that possible costs should be secondary. "Our notoriously lax attitude toward illegal immigration," says Peter Salins, "sends the message that we do not care enough about who we are as a nation even to enforce our own laws." [105] Others disagree, assessing the costs as prohibitive and the ultimate goal as much less important than its proponents believe. The debate over managing illegal immigration touches on questions of privacy, the use of the military, and taxes. In short, it asks how a democratic country can achieve consensus on an extremely divisive issue.

At least one observer believes Americans have done all that can ethically be done. "The [Border] Patrol," writes Sebastian Rotella, has "achieved the modest results that were permitted by the self-imposed restraints of a democratic society. The border could not be sealed," Rotella admits, "but the illegal flow of people could be managed and discouraged." [106] In his view, it has. The compromise may not be entirely comfortable for most citizens; in particular, it may not satisfy advocates on either side of the issue. But Rotella's basic point may well be right: Politically, the United States can neither crack down much further on illegal immigrants nor let up much more on enforcement. For better or worse, the current situation may be the only politically tenable solution.

Should Immigration Policy Be Reformed?

IN MAY 1998, MARTINIQUE-BORN David Regis became a naturalized American citizen. Unlike most other new citizens, who typically spend years as legal immigrants in the United States before qualifying for the naturalization process, Regis had barely lived in the United States at all. Also unlike most other new citizens, Regis spoke almost no English.

Yet Regis succeeded in gaining admission to the United States—and even becoming a citizen—when thousands of others fail. The reason? Regis was a talented soccer player. His admission to the country was specifically designed to shore up a relatively weak U.S. national team in the 1998 World Cup soccer tournament. Team officials arranged for Regis's wife, a U.S. citizen herself, to be given a one-year job with an American company engaged in international trade. Under current immigration rules, an American national who takes such a post may have his or her spouse apply immediately for immigrant and citizen status. Regis took full advantage of the rule. Less than six months later, Regis was officially naturalized.

On the Fast Track

David Regis is far from the only athlete for whom American immigration and naturalization laws have been conveniently bent. Several of Regis's teammates were given similar preferential treatment. Roy Wegerle, born in South Africa, is one example; his wife was given a job by a World Cup organizing committee so he could play for the national team. Reserve David Wagner of Germany is another. Although Wagner lists his residence as Los Angeles he spends virtually no time there outside soccer season. The trend is evident in other sports, too. As of this writing, for instance, Moroccan distance runner Khalid Khannouchi is trying to gain citizenship in time to compete as an American in the 2000 Olympics.

Putting athletes on the fast track to immigration and citizenship has its defenders. The United States ought to be able to field the best athletic teams possible, say some. If that means bringing in athletes from other countries, so be it. Some also point out that Regis, Wegerle, and others all have gone through perfectly legal channels,

Moroccan distance runner Khalid Khannouchi hopes to gain U.S. citizenship in time to compete as an American in the 2000 Olympics.

channels open in theory to any would-be immigrant. And some argue that many of these athletes are truly interested in becoming American. "The United States is something special," says Khannouchi. "I want to die for the American flag one day."[107]

Others, however, are less certain. U.S. representative Lamar Smith, chair of an immigration subcommittee, opposes Khannouchi's request. "It would be unfair to expedite naturalization," Smith argues, "to allow [someone] to compete against American citizens for the small amount of slots on the U.S. Olympic team."[108] Some athletes feel the same way. A U.S. soccer player opposed Regis's quick path to citizenship on much the same grounds. Allowing Regis onto the national team, he says, not only deprived some native-born Americans of playing time during the World Cup tournament, but took a roster spot away from a deserving player as well.

The concern about fairness, however, runs deeper than concern for U.S.-born athletes denied opportunities to compete. A more basic issue is involved. Taking special steps to bring in a few chosen people, athletes or no, smacks of favoritism. For many, perhaps most Americans, Regis and Khannouchi are no more deserving than are thousands of other foreigners anxious, even desperate, to become Americans. To give them special treatment, merely because they have athletic skills, seems to run counter to the notion that all prospective immigrants are equal.

The Odds of Gaining Entry

But, in fact, the United States does not consider all prospective immigrants equally. U.S. immigration policy is not a single lottery system in which all would-be immigrants have identical odds of winning the prize. It is a good deal more complicated than that. Each immigrant, in essence, explains why he or she ought to be admitted, with justifications ranging from particular job skills to chaos in the country of origin. Those who claim job skills are put in one category, those with family ties to U.S. citizens in another, refugees in a third. Within each category, prospective immigrants compete for the privilege of entering the United States. Instead of one lottery system, therefore, there are several.

Because the odds of gaining entry vary depending on the category, immigration policy has the effect of encouraging certain types of immigrants while discouraging others. Unfortunately, making immigration easy for some while turning away others leads to controversy. Some argue passionately for more openness in admitting certain kinds of immigrants; others argue just as passionately for keeping the numbers in that category down, but loosening or even eliminating restrictions elsewhere. The problem is complex. Many different people want to come to America for many different reasons under very different circumstances. Finding a fair way to compare the needs of political refugees, family members of citizens, and skilled workers is hard indeed.

Categories

Today, there are four major categories by which immigrants may legally enter the United States. These categories are often known as preferences. The first, and most common, is being the immediate family member—the spouse, parent, or minor son or daughter—of a current U.S. citizen or a permanent resident alien. In 1996, for

In 1998, U.S. Army corporal Adam Cook asked the Immigration and Naturalization Service to permit his German-born wife and their two children to stay with him in the United States.

instance, 300,000 new immigrants arrived under this provision. A close second is being a more distant relative, especially an adult child or an adult brother or sister of a current U.S. citizen. In 1996, 294,000 people entered the United States under this so-called relative preference. Together, family preferences account for nearly two-thirds of the total numbers of immigrants.

The other two major categories are less common. About a sixth of new immigrants each year are refugees or asylees—that is, people facing a serious danger in their own country. These people are distributed much more narrowly among home countries than are some other immigrants. In 1996, for example, about three-fifths of refugees came from just four nations: Vietnam, Cuba, Russia, and Ukraine. And the remaining sixth of immigrants comes in annually under the "occupational preference" heading. They have job skills needed by American corporations, skills not widely available among U.S. citizens. Of all four ways of getting into the United States, the occupational preference category is the most strictly limited.

Family Reunification

The limits—or lack of limits—placed on these preferences have come under heavy fire during the last few years. The family categories have been especially controversial. Most of the criticism has been leveled at the policy that permits extended family members of recent immigrants to come into the United States. Many Americans, while sympathetic to the desires of immigrants to bring in adult children, adult siblings, and parents, wonder whether the policy is being abused. Peter Salins calls family reunification "a superficially attractive criterion,"[109] but like many others Salins believes that the principle creates problems for the United States.

One effect of family preference has been to lower the skill levels of immigrants. In theory any American with extended family overseas can bring them in under this preference. In practice, however, those family members with high skills tend to stay put; they are usually doing well enough where they are. Immigration has proved much more appealing to family members with little education, few job skills, and a dim future. As a result, a large percentage of those admitted under family preference are poorly skilled. Many observers feel that this practice makes little sense. "An illiterate laborer with no skills, but with a parent in the United States," points out a journalist, "has a better shot at immigration than does a graduate-school-educated foreigner with no family or employer here."[110] Many Americans would prefer the immigrant with the degree, and doubt that choosing the laborer is in the best interest of the country.

Others see a hidden quota system in family preference. The various family preferences account for a good chunk of all immigrants permitted every year. Members of large immigrant groups, by bringing in family members, can ensure that their communities grow quickly. Other, less numerous immigrant groups can grow, too, but because they are starting from a less numerous base, that growth is much more gradual. This tends to preserve the current distribution of immigrants by country of origin, whether doing so makes sense for the United States or not. Family reunification, says a magazine editorial, "has allowed a handful of Third World countries to shoulder everyone else aside and claim the bulk of legal immigration slots."[111]

Still others question whether family preference categories are truly necessary. "The immigrants . . . made the decision to separate from their families by coming here," points out Roy Beck. "Nobody forced them. If they have a passionate need to live near their relatives, they should move back."[112] Beck acknowledges the importance of reuniting husbands with wives and parents with minor children, but he believes that all other forms of family reunification—including bringing elderly parents into the United States—should be stopped.

A few people do support family reunification as presently constituted. Current policy reflects the cultural connections many Third World immigrants feel to their more distant relatives, connections which in some cases equal what Americans feel for their closest kin. Some studies suggest that extended families help smooth the transition to America for workers. Others have found that members of extended immigrant families are less likely to be impoverished than are similar families who arrive on their own. And several ethnic organizations have lobbied for continued family preferences. The National Council of La Raza, for example, a Hispanic advocacy group, has been a strong supporter of keeping current policy; family unification is a strong concern of many Hispanic Americans. But criticism of the family reunification preference has outweighed support in recent years.

Skilled Workers

The occupational preference has also been controversial; indeed, it has been attacked from both sides. At present about 150,000 slots are available every year under this preference. Those who believe that Americans can handle most jobs would eliminate the preference altogether, or very nearly so. "If there is dogged unemployment," points out a critic of this policy, "there is no manifest need for more labor."[113] Since not all Americans have jobs, so this argument runs, it is foolishness to bring in more workers from outside the United States.

But others argue the point. To them, the numbers arriving under occupational preferences are far too low. "58 percent of companies face a skilled worker shortage today," says a writer, "compared to 28 percent three years ago."[114] Businesses often complain that they cannot hire enough engineers, programmers, and others with technical skills. Refusing to extend the occupational preference, in this view, is foolishness; it simply has the effect of making U.S. corporations fall behind the rest of the world. In recent years business interests have successfully lobbied for increases in the skills quota; still, it lags well behind the family preference category.

Refugees

Given the concerns many Americans have about immigrants taking American jobs, opposition to the employment of skills preference might be expected. In contrast, the preferences regarding refugees and asylees might seem uncontroversial. After all, the world can be a very dangerous place. Natural disasters, economic collapse, political squabbles, wars—all lead to massive dislocations as people try to escape chaos. The United States is widely considered a desirable safe haven for these refugees. It has served as such frequently in the past, too—more often than any other nation, and by quite a large margin. "We can, and should, keep our doors open to the oppressed of other lands," writes one observer.[115]

*A Cuban refugee
gazes at the ocean as
a ship transports him
to the United States.*

But debate over refugees is nevertheless intense. Unfortunately, many who have lately come seeking refuge are not at all needy. "Some use the asylum system as a means simply to get a work permit," admits the commissioner of the INS.[116] The process relies on would-be refugees telling the truth about themselves. Immigrants need not even have papers to prove they are who they say they are, since a legitimate refugee might have to leave home in a hurry; unfortunately, this makes the process ripe for fraud. Asylees need only say they come from any of nearly 150 countries which, according to human rights organizations, mistreats its citizens. The result has too often been immigrants' gaining admission to the United States through unfair means. For this reason, some would limit the numbers of immigrants admitted as refugees every year.

Others, in contrast, fear that the designation of refugee is awarded all too infrequently. Some charge that refugee status has mainly to do with political considerations. Asylum seekers from leftist nations have traditionally been much more likely to receive refugee status than those from rightist dictatorships. "No regime in Haiti is ever murderous enough to make more Haitians eligible as refugees," charges Peter Salins, "and no African country's policies of persecution or mutilation are ever cruel enough to make Africans eligible as asylees, but as long as Fidel Castro is in power, Cubans will continue to be welcome."[117] In this view, the policy of extending admission to those in need has been perverted into a method of showing distaste for certain regimes while supporting others. The designation of "refugee" needs to be broadened, Salins and others agree.

Too Many Immigrants?

Numbers have also been controversial in the immigration reform debate. Many observers believe the United States can no longer accept all those who seek a better life. There are simply too many immigrants today. Some worry about the effect of immigrants on jobs, on services, and on the national culture. Others worry about crime, poverty, and the environment. Whatever the specifics, many Americans fear that U.S. society has reached the limit of its ability to absorb newcomers. Simply put, the country has space for only so many people, and that limit has been reached.

There is little doubt that immigration is driving current population growth. Birth rates among native-born Americans have dropped to very low levels; child-bearing women born in the United States are barely producing enough offspring to replace their own generation. Moreover, as the native population grows older, the percentage of children in the United States is bound to shrink. Immigration changes that. In the 1990s, demographers say, immigration had accounted for just about half the total population growth of the United States. Add in children born here to immigrants, and the percentage is even higher. Without immigration, population growth in the United States would be moving slowly indeed.

With immigration, on the other hand, population continues to rise at a quick pace. Immigrants, in fact, have a double effect on

Because of mass IMMIGRATION, U.S. population will exceed half a BILLION in my lifetime. Help us, Congress.
— an American kid, age 6
www.ProjectUSA.org
Source: U.S. Census Bureau

An anti-immigration billboard asserts that mass immigration will result in overpopulation.

population. First, they add to the numbers simply by coming to this country. Second, they tend to have more children than native-born Americans, which further swells the population. And if those children continue to reproduce at a higher rate when they reach adulthood, the pattern is clear: One immigrant couple today will likely have many more grandchildren and great-grandchildren than a typical native-born couple. Add that to the number of new immigrants due to arrive each year, and immigration's effect on population could be significant.

How significant remains to be seen, however. Some demographers project a constant rise in the number of Americans, with the rate of increase picking up sharply in the early years of the twenty-first century. Many experts estimate that U.S. population in 2030 will be approximately 350 million—an increase of 100 million in less than forty years, virtually all due to immigrants and their descendants.

For some, this presents a dangerous picture. That figure may simply be too many people for the country. One common concern regarding this number is ecological. The current U.S. population already puts tremendous pressures on the environment; the effects of another 100 million may overwhelm natural resources. As a result, several environmental organizations have come out in favor of limits on immigration. "Population policy should protect and sustain ecological systems for future generations," reads the Wilderness Society's 1996 mission statement. "To bring population levels to ecologically sustainable levels, both birthrates and immigration rates need to be reduced."[118]

Human depletion of resources is another issue. There is no guarantee that we can feed an extra hundred million mouths, warn some experts. Water is already running short in dozens of communities. Cities may become unimaginably crowded, as densely packed as they were in earlier times of high immigration. Pressures on the buildings, bridges, and sewer systems that serve society are of particular concern. Many cities cannot repair broken water mains; some communities are far behind when it comes to building schools. "Texas needs to complete two schools every week—indefinitely—to keep up," points out Roy Beck. "Who is going to pay for all the classrooms?"[119]

Concerns about resources, population density, and the environment, combined with questions about immigrants' effect on jobs and welfare systems, lead many observers to recommend that immigration levels be cut. Suggested limits range from six hundred thousand or so a year—about two-thirds of the current legal total—down to near zero. These views have garnered some support among Americans. "More than 8 out of 10 Americans want immigration drastically reduced or stopped altogether," says one anti-immigrant organization.[120] A 1996 poll found widespread support for reducing immigration to less than one hundred thousand a year—about a tenth of current levels. Even among relatively recent immigrants there is support for cutbacks. A 1990 survey revealed that three-quarters of Mexican Americans and even higher numbers of Puerto Ricans agreed with the statement "There are too many immigrants coming to this country."[121]

Immigration Advocates

Not all observers accept these recommendations, however. Pro-immigration advocates dispute the population statistics offered by

Heavy traffic clogs a freeway. Opponents of immigration claim that increased immigration stresses natural resources and the environment.

those who wish to reduce the totals of newcomers. The U.S. population, they point out, is far larger today than it was a hundred years ago. Thus, immigration represents a much smaller percentage of the total now than it once did. Immigrants of the 1990s represented little more than 3 percent of the population, a lower percentage than in every decade from 1840 to 1930. In this view, since the United

States has successfully accommodated earlier immigrants, it should have no trouble accommodating a much smaller proportion today.

Nor do advocates see a high population as a major issue in itself. Urban sprawl and other environmental concerns, though fueled in part by population growth, are fundamentally the result of lifestyle choices, not excessive immigration. "The size of the population isn't the problem," say leaders of the Sierra Club, which voted down an anti-immigrant resolution. "It's the rate at which we consume the world's forests, fuel, fish and other finite resources."[122] Laws restricting development, together with public acceptance of mass transit, energy conservation, and a less wasteful way of life, would help the environment much more than immigrants hurt it, especially as immigrants, poorer than the general population, tend to use fewer resources than the native population anyway.

Besides, proponents of immigration argue, projections that show population rising out of control are nothing but educated guesses. Some demographers predict that U.S. population will grow much more slowly, even with high immigration levels. Similarly, several projections say that population will diminish if immigration is drastically lowered. "With the dramatic decline in its birth rates and fertility rates," says one source, "the U.S. might very well begin to experience negative population growth by the year 2030."[123] Population declines present economic problems of their own—supporting an increasingly elderly population and finding workers to run businesses are only two of many.

Thus, pro-immigrant thinkers typically believe that the number of immigrants is either about right or, in some cases, not nearly enough. "This country needs more, not fewer, immigrants," says Julian Simon. "The U.S. birthrate is low and our future work force is shrinking."[124] Though few supporters of immigration pin themselves to a specific number, most agree that the principle of increased immigration makes sense.

Recommendations

Controversies over numbers and process have inspired numerous suggestions for reforming the way immigrants are chosen. Some of these suggestions close loopholes or make minor reforms: tightening the asylum-seeking process, for example, to winnow out abuse of the system by those not in true need, or dropping the most distant of relatives from the family preference categories. Others are more sweeping. Some probusiness writers urge an unlimited number of immigration slots for workers needed by U.S. companies. And Roy Beck would allow virtually no one to immigrate but immediate family members of U.S. citizens. Each approach has adherents and detractors.

A few thinkers, however, believe that the system itself is the problem. Other countries that take relatively high numbers of immigrants, such as Canada and Australia, use different systems to determine who gets in. Canada, for example, awards would-be immigrants a certain number of points for desirable characteristics—so many for knowledge of English or French, so many more for levels of education. Points are also awarded in varying amounts for job skills, age, and the presence in Canada of family members. A perfect score is 100, but 100 points does not necessarily guarantee admission. Canadian policy accepts varying numbers of immigrants each year depending on the needs of the nation.

Immigrants from Hong Kong receive language and cultural help from volunteers in a Canadian hospital.

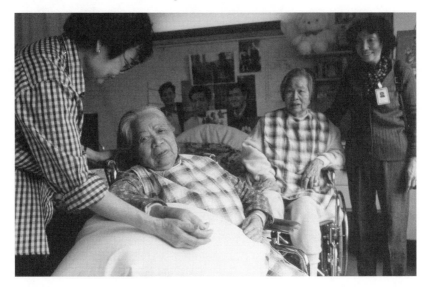

Many observers believe that the United States should adopt such a system. It may well be in America's best interest to vary the number of immigrants each year according to the country's perceived need. A point system also helps Americans move away from the question of limits and toward the question of what we want, focusing not so much on whether immigration itself is good or bad, but on which aspects of immigration are positive and which negative. A point system would allow the government to make worthwhile distinctions between immigrants. Those who will most help the country, whether economically or culturally, will receive more points, and those whose presence is more a burden than a benefit will receive lower totals.

Of course, point systems are themselves controversial. The idea of judging which characteristics are worth more than others makes some uncomfortable. Others dislike the notion because a point system implies a cap on the skilled-laborer category or the family-reunification heading. One proposal, by researchers Kevin McCarthy and Georges Vernez, tries to change the current system only marginally: It maintains the notion of family reunification, for example, but awards fewer points for extended family than it awards for other characteristics. As a journalist describes the plan, "a college-educated computer programmer with no family would get in before an educated laborer with siblings."[125] Americans may ultimately decide that the reverse should instead be true, but a point system provides a good starting point for discussion of what works and what does not.

There are other proposals. One writer suggests selling immigration slots to the highest bidder. This system would simultaneously benefit the U.S. Treasury and make sure that those who came were able to support themselves. Moreover, people already in the United States could pay the fees for would-be immigrants, so corporations looking for skilled workers or citizens wishing family members to join them would be able to make their preferences known. Prospective immigrants who have neither a sponsor nor the necessary funds could perhaps take out some kind of government loan to pay their way. A scheme like this, say proponents, will "reduce the hostility toward new immigrants and toward policies that do not reduce rates

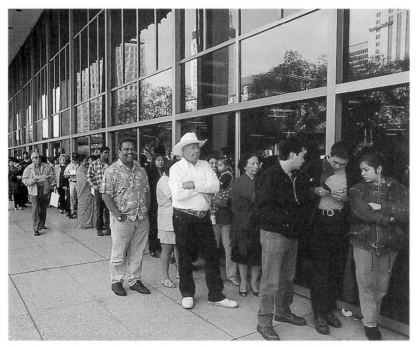

Immigrants in Los Angeles line up for green card applications. Proponents of immigration believe immigrants help stimulate the U.S. economy and help create a new and stronger culture.

of immigration."[126] Others disagree, viewing the sale of immigration slots as ripe for corruption, at odds with U.S. history and tradition, and not consistent with the U.S. role as a strong and welcoming nation for all who seek a better life.

In the long run the debate over which people should be permitted to come to this country reflects the larger debate over immigration. Those observers who want to limit immigration and eliminate some preference categories tend to be the same people who fear that immigrants are taking jobs away from Americans, overburdening the social services system, and refusing to assimilate. Those arguing for expanded preference categories, however, are usually those who see immigrants as adding to the U.S. economy and helping to create a new and stronger culture.

Certainly both sides have valid arguments and concerns. There is statistical and anecdotal evidence available to support the notion that immigration is bad for the United States; there is also evidence to support the opposite claim. It would be too much to expect the two sides to agree on a particular immigration policy for the United States. Nevertheless, the two sides—and the United States as a whole—can benefit from listening carefully to each other's concerns and arguments and by viewing the available evidence dispassionately.

The face of immigration today is not the same as it was a hundred years ago, nor even the same as it was fifty years ago. The United States has changed. So has the world that surrounds it. Policies that were effective for Germans arriving in 1848 may not work for Mexicans arriving in 2010. Immigration laws that helped designate who could and could not enter had one kind of impact when nearly all immigrants had to cross an ocean by ship in order to get here, but may mean something very different when the rest of the world is less than eighteen hours away by plane. The overall goals for immigration are necessarily different for a settled twenty-first century population than they were for a young nation still expanding over its territory. The question for the future is to determine whether, and how, the United States will best benefit from immigration. To hear and respect all sides of the debate will help immeasurably in finding these answers and putting them into effect.

NOTES

Chapter 1: Should Assimilation Be a Priority for Immigrants?

1. Quoted in Thaddeus Herrick, "Spanish Official Language in 'Safe-Haven' Border City," *Houston Chronicle*, August 14, 1999, p. 1+.
2. Quoted in Herrick, "Spanish Official Language in 'Safe-Haven' Border City," p. 1+.
3. Quoted in Herrick, "Spanish Official Language in 'Safe-Haven' Border City," p. 1+.
4. Quoted in Herrick, "Spanish Official Language in 'Safe-Haven' Border City," p. 1+.
5. Quoted in Scott Baldauf, "In This City Hall, Official Business Is in Spanish," *Christian Science Monitor*, August 25, 1999, p. 1+.
6. Quoted in Baldauf, "In This City Hall, Official Business Is in Spanish," p. 1+.
7. Quoted in Tamara Roleff, ed., *Immigration*. San Diego: Greenhaven Press, 1998, p. 197.
8. Peter D. Salins, "Assimilation, American Style," *Reason,* February 1997, p. 22.
9. Quoted in William Scott Barbour, ed., *Illegal Immigration*. San Diego: Greenhaven Press, 1994, p. 48.
10. Quoted in Bill Bryson, *Made in America*. New York: Avon Books, 1994, p. 143.
11. Quoted in Salins, "Assimilation, American Style," p. 20.
12. Quoted in William Scott Barbour, ed., *Immigration Policy*. San Diego: Greenhaven Press, 1995, p. 32.
13. Peter Brimelow, "Un-American Activities," *National Review,* June 16, 1997, p. 44.

14. Salins, "Assimilation, American Style," p. 26.
15. Quoted in Scott McConnell, "Americans No More?" *National Review*, December 31, 1997, p. 33.
16. Quoted in McConnell, "Americans No More?" p. 30.
17. Quoted in Barbour, *Illegal Immigration,* p. 23.
18. Quoted in Barbour, *Illegal Immigration*, pp. 47–48.
19. Ron French and Christopher M. Singer, "Newcomers Challenge Traditional Hamtramck," *Detroit News*, June 14, 1999, p. A1+.
20. Quoted in Sheba R. Wheeler, "Hmong Parents Strive to Connect," *Denver Post*, November 15, 1998, p. B1+.
21. Daniela Deane, "Promised Land Yields Bitter Fruit for Some," *USA Today*, October 7, 1998, p. 10A+.
22. Quoted in Deane, "Promised Land Yields Bitter Fruit for Some," p. 10A+.
23. Quoted in Roleff, *Immigration*, p. 115.
24. Quoted in David Brauer, "Twin Cities Radio Station Bows to Hmongs' Pressure," *Chicago Tribune*, November 6, 1998, p. 12.
25. Salins, "Assimilation, American-Style," p. 25.
26. "*Economist*, The Melting Pot Survives," July 3, 1999, p. 24+.
27. "Melting Pot Bubbling Along," *Los Angeles Times*, August 2, 1999, p. 4+.
28. Thomas Kessner and Betty Boyd Carroll, *Today's Immigrants: Their Stories.* New York: Oxford University Press, 1982, p. 235.
29. Quoted in Bryson, *Made in America,* p. 140.
30. "The Melting Pot Survives," p. 24+.
31. Quoted in "Melting Pot Bubbling Along," p. 4+.
32. Quoted in Kessner and Carroll, *Today's Immigrants*, p. 146.
33. Abigail McCarthy, "The New Immigrants," *Commonweal,* April 24, 1998, p. 9.
34. Bryson, *Made in America,* p. 364.

Chapter 2: Does Immigration Harm U.S. Workers?

35. Quoted in Roy Beck, *The Case Against Immigration.* New York: W. W. Norton, 1996, p. 105.
36. Marc Cooper, "The Heartland's Raw Deal," *Nation*, February 3, 1997, p. 15.
37. Quoted in Beck, *The Case Against Immigration,* p. 100.
38. Cooper, "The Heartland's Raw Deal," p. 15.

39. Beck, *The Case Against Immigration,* p. 111.

40. Quoted in Roleff, *Immigration,* p. 76.

41. Ronald Steel, "The Bad News," *New Republic,* February 10, 1997, p. 27.

42. Quoted in Steven Anzovin, ed., *The Problem of Immigration.* New York: H. W. Wilson, 1985, p. 29.

43. Quoted in Charles P. Cozic, ed., *Illegal Immigration.* San Diego: Greenhaven Press, 1997, p. 76.

44. Quoted in Barbour, *Immigration Policy,* p. 61.

45. David Warner, "Reaching the Limit on Worker Visas," *Nation's Business,* August 1998, p. 27.

46. Quoted in Barbour, *Immigration Policy,* p. 60.

47. Quoted in Michael Lind, "Hiring from Within," *Mother Jones,* July/August 1998, p. 61.

48. Quoted in Dan Mihalopoulos, "Growing Beyond the Melting Pot," *St. Louis Post-Dispatch,* May 9, 1999, p. B1+.

49. Quoted in Howard Gleckman, "High-Tech Talent: Don't Bolt the Golden Door," *Business Week,* March 16, 1998, p. 30.

50. Quoted in John Cassidy, "The Melting-Pot Myth," *New Yorker,* July 14, 1997, p. 40.

51. Quoted in Mihalopoulos, "Growing Beyond the Melting Pot," p. B1+.

52. Quoted in Alison Landes et al., eds., *Immigration and Illegal Aliens: Burden or Blessing?* Wylie, TX: Information Plus, 1993, p. 111.

53. Quoted in Anzovin, *The Problem of Immigration,* p. 109

54. Lind, "Hiring from Within," p. 61.

55. Cooper, "The Heartland's Raw Deal," p. 15.

56. Steel, "The Bad News," p. 27.

57. Quoted in Cassidy, "The Melting-Pot Myth," p. 41.

58. Quoted in Barbour, *Illegal Immigration,* p. 70.

59. Quoted in Lind, "Hiring from Within," p. 62.

60. Gleckman, "High-Tech Talent," p. 30.

61. Quoted in Kessner and Carroll, *Today's Immigrants,* p. 13.

Chapter 3: Should Immigrants Be Denied Access to Government Services?

62. Quoted in Cassidy, "The Melting-Pot Myth," p. 40.

63. Dan Stein, "Immigration Is Fueling Poverty Rate," *Los Angeles*

Times, July 6, 1999, p. 5.

64. Quoted in Anzovin, *The Problem of Immigration,* p. 130.

65. Quoted in Cozic, *Illegal Immigration,* p. 30.

66. Quoted in Ruth Conniff, "Going Hungry," *Progressive,* July 1998, p. 9.

67. George Borjas, "Immigration & Welfare," *National Review,* June 16, 1997, p. 35.

68. Quoted in Cozic, *Illegal Immigration,* p. 95.

69. Quoted in Conniff, "Going Hungry," p. 9.

70. Quoted in Cozic, *Illegal Immigration,* p. 39.

71. Quoted in Patrick J. McDonnell, "State OKs Prenatal Aid for Immigrants," *Los Angeles Times,* July 27, 1999.

72. Quoted in Cozic, *Illegal Immigration,* p. 87.

73. Quoted in Paul Glastris, "The Alien Payoff," *U.S. News & World Report,* May 26, 1997, p. 20.

74. Quoted in Glastris, "The Alien Payoff," p. 21.

75. "Legal and Fearful Too," *Los Angeles Times,* June 4, 1997, p. 6.

76. Linda Chavez, "Debunking the Illegal-Immigrant Welfare Myth," *Denver Post,* March 17, 1999, p. B11.

77. Ramon G. McLeod, "Why Proposed Crackdowns on Immigrants Never Happened," *San Francisco Chronicle,* October 16, 1998, p. A6.

78. Esther Schrader, "GOP's Muted Response to Welfare Plan Is a Telling Sign of the Times," *Los Angeles Times,* February 8, 1999, p. 6+.

Chapter 4: Should Efforts to Halt Illegal Immigration Be Strengthened?

79. Quoted in Carol Morello, "Living in Fear on the Border," *USA Today,* July 21, 1999, p. 1A+.

80. August Gribbin, "Alien Invasion Alarms Arizonans," *Washington Times,* June 7, 1999, p. 42.

81. Quoted in Morello, "Living in Fear on the Border," p. 1A+.

82. Quoted in Sean Paige, "Raiding Arizona," *Washington Times,* July 26, 1999, p. 10+.

83. Quoted in Paige, "Raiding Arizona, p. 10+.

84. Quoted in Landes et al., *Immigration and Illegal Aliens,* p. 84.

85. Marcus Stern, "Withering Wages," *San Diego Union-Tribune,*

August 23, 1999, p. A1+.

86. Quoted in Kessner and Carroll, *Today's Immigrants,* p. 80.

87. Quoted in Cozic, *Illegal Immigration,* p. 146.

88. Quoted in Gordon Witkin, "One Way, $28,000," *U.S. News & World Report,* April 14, 1997, p. 41.

89. Quoted in Sebastian Rotella, *Twilight on the Line.* New York: W. W. Norton, 1998, p. 87.

90. Quoted in Landes et al., *Immigration and Illegal Aliens,* p. 95.

91. Quoted in Chitra Ragavan and Douglas Pasternak, "A Borderline Cop Shop?" *U.S. News & World Report,* July 19, 1999, p. 22.

92. Quoted in Witkin, "One Way, $28,000," p. 41.

93. Quoted in Kessner and Carroll, *Today's Immigrants,* p. 82.

94. Quoted in Rotella, *Twilight on the Line,* p. 51.

95. Quoted in Cozic, *Illegal Immigration,* p. 115.

96. Quoted in Morello, "Living in Fear on the Border," p. 1A+.

97. Quoted in Cozic, *Illegal Immigration,* p. 148.

98. Quoted in Rotella, *Twilight on the Line,* p. 64.

99. Rotella, *Twilight on the Line,* p. 33.

100. Quoted in Kessner and Carroll, *Today's Immigrants,* p. 81.

101. Quoted in Daniel W. Sutherland, "Identity Crisis," *Reason,* December 1997, p. 63.

102. Sutherland, "Identity Crisis," p. 63.

103. Rotella, *Twilight on the Line,* p. 61.

104. Viva Hardigg, "When Prop. 187 Comes to the Classroom," *U.S. News & World Report,* February 3, 1997, p. 50.

105. Peter D. Salins, "Towards a New Immigration Policy," *Commentary,* January 1997, p. 47.

106. Rotella, *Twilight on the Line,* p. 127.

Chapter 5: Should Immigration Policy Be Reformed?

107. Quoted in Dick Patrick, "Khannouchi Chases His American Dream," *USA Today,* October 1, 1998, p. 4E.

108. Quoted in "The Khannouchi Case," *Runner's World,* June 1999, p. 20.

109. Salins, "Towards a New Immigration Policy," p. 47.

110. Susan Headden, "Favor Aliens with Job Skills," *U.S. News & World Report,* December 29, 1997–January 5, 1998, p. 84.

111. "Give Me—Everybody," *National Review,* December 31,

1997, p. 16.

112. Beck, *The Case Against Immigration,* p. 253.

113. William F. Buckley Jr., "Squabbling on the Right," *National Review,* February 24, 1997, p. 62.

114. John J. Miller, "The Politics of Permanent Immigration," *Reason,* October 1998, p. 38.

115. Steel, "The Bad News," p. 27.

116. Quoted in Barbour, *Immigration Policy,* p. 29.

117. Quoted in Roleff, *Immigration,* p. 173.

118. Quoted in Dick Schneider and Alan Kuper, "Why We Need a Comprehensive U.S. Population Policy," *Sierra,* January/February 1998, p. 105.

119. Beck, *The Case Against Immigration,* p. 210.

120. FAIR, "Immigration: Kennedy Got It Half Right," *National Review,* June 16, 1997, p. 33.

121. Quoted in Lind, "Hiring from Within," p. 62.

122. Quoted in Greg Goldin, "The Greening of Hate," *Nation,* May 18, 1998, p. 7.

123. John W. Wright, ed., *1999 New York Times Almanac.* New York: Penguin, 1998, p. 292.

124. Quoted in Anzovin, *The Problem of Immigration,* p. 131.

125. Headden, "Favor Aliens with Job Skills," p. 84.

126. Quoted in Roleff, *Immigration,* p. 178.

ORGANIZATIONS TO CONTACT

Center for Immigration Studies
1522 K St. NW, Suite 820
Washington, DC 20005-1202
phone: 202-466-8185
e-mail: center@cis.org
website: http://www.cis.org.cis

The center investigates and analyzes the various effects of immigration on America. Also publishes brochures and journals.

Federation for American Immigration Reform
1666 Connecticut Ave. NW
Washington, DC 20009
phone: 202-328-7004
email: info@fairus.org
website: http://www.fairus.org

Dedicated to stopping illegal immigration entirely and severely restricting the numbers of legal immigrants. Publishes position papers and reports.

Immigration and Naturalization Service
Department of Justice
Constitution Ave. and 10th St. NW
Washington, DC 20530
phone: 202-514-2000
website: www.ins.usdoj.gov

The INS is in charge of enforcing immigration policy within the United States. The Border Patrol is an arm of the service.

National Immigration Forum
220 I St. NE, Suite 220
Washington, DC 20002-4362
phone: 202-544-0004
website: www.immigrationforum.org

A pro-immigration group that sees immigrants as strengthening, not harming, the United States. Works for assimilation and against illegal immigration.

National Network for Immigrant and Refugee Rights
310 Eighth St., Suite 307
Oakland, CA 94607-4253
phone: 510-465-1984
e-mail: nnirr@nnirr.org
website: http://www.nnirr.org

An umbrella organization of several groups that work to guarantee fair treatment for all immigrants, especially those here as refugees or as illegal immigrants.

Negative Population Growth, Inc.
1717 Massachusetts Ave. NW, Suite 101
Washington, DC 20036
e-mail: npg@npg.org
website: http://www.npg.org

The organization believes that the United States is already badly overpopulated and advocates strictly reducing immigration of all kinds to 200,000 a year.

FOR FURTHER READING

Steven Anzovin, ed., *The Problem of Immigration.* New York: H. W. Wilson, 1985. Readings about immigration issues, mostly taken from the popular press. Particularly interested in refugees, policy, and illegal aliens.

William Scott Barbour, ed., *Illegal Immigration.* San Diego: Greenhaven Press, 1994. A title in the Current Controversies series. Readings cover all aspects of illegal immigration, from politics and policy to hardships and welfare.

————, *Immigration Policy.* San Diego: Greenhaven Press, 1995. Eighteen viewpoints on what U.S. immigration policy should look like. A good mix of perspectives and authors.

Julie Catalano, *Mexican Americans.* Broomall, PA: Chelsea House, 1995. Part of the Immigrant Experience series, this book details the lives of past and present immigrants from Mexico.

Vic Cox, *The Challenge of Immigration.* Springfield, NJ: Enslow, 1995. A discussion of the debates surrounding ethnicity, illegal immigrants, and more.

Charles P. Cozic, ed., *Illegal Immigration.* San Diego: Greenhaven Press, 1997. Readings dealing with illegal aliens and their impact on American society.

Meish Goldish, *Immigration: How Should It Be Controlled?* New York: Twenty-First Century Books, 1995. A short discussion of the questions surrounding immigration, with special focus on how—and whether—immigration should be limited.

Thomas Kessner and Betty Boyd Carroll, *Today's Immigrants:*

99

Their Stories. New York: Oxford University Press, 1982. Interviews and summaries of discussions with New York City immigrants. Personal narratives of immigrants' lives are punctuated by information about the topics in this book.

Robert Morrow, *Immigration: Blessing or Burden.* Minneapolis: Lerner, 1997. A discussion of the pros and cons of large-scale immigration.

Tamara Roleff, ed., *Immigration.* San Diego: Greenhaven Press, 1998. A title in the Opposing Viewpoints series. Clear, readable articles and book excerpts, most relating to the controversies in this book. Includes historical background.

WORKS CONSULTED

Books

Michael Barone and Grant Ujifusa, *The Almanac of American Politics 2000.* Washington, DC: National Journal, 1999. The essential book on current American government, with profiles of House and Senate members and their districts. Several sections refer to the immigration controversy.

Roy Beck, *The Case Against Immigration.* New York: W. W. Norton, 1996. A thoughtful attack on current immigration policy. For reasons of jobs, environment, and more, Beck would drastically cut immigration.

Peter Brimelow, *Alien Invasion: Common Sense About America's Immigration Disaster.* New York: Random House, 1995. Brimelow, a leading voice against immigration, outlines his case in this book.

Bill Bryson, *Made in America.* New York: Avon Books, 1994. A very readable history of the English language in the United States. Bryson discusses immigrants and their effect on the language; throughout, he takes the long view.

Georgie Anne Geyer, *Americans No More.* New York: Atlantic Monthly Press, 1996. Geyer, a syndicated columnist, expresses her concerns about the effect of today's open immigration policies.

David Jacobson, *Rights Across Borders: Immigration and the Decline of Citizenship.* Baltimore: Johns Hopkins University Press, 1998. A study of the way international borders have become less of a barrier in recent years; a good deal of information about immigration on a global scale.

Alison Landes et al., eds., *Immigration and Illegal Aliens: Burden or Blessing?* Wylie, TX: Information Plus, 1993. Thorough and full of statistics, this book examines the issues of refugees, illegal aliens, assimilation, and more.

Joel Millman, *The Other Americans: How Immigrants Renew Our Country, Our Economy, and Our Values.* New York: Viking, 1997. An expression of the pro-immigrant perspective.

Sebastian Rotella, *Twilight on the Line.* New York: W. W. Norton, 1998. A journalist's account of the California-Mexico border. Much of the book centers on the issue of illegal immigration, though other topics are covered.

John W. Wright, ed., *1999 New York Times Almanac.* New York: Penguin, 1998. Includes statistics and a brief discussion of the issues surrounding immigration today.

Periodicals

"Asides: Tex-Mex Tensions," *Wall Street Journal*, August 16, 1999.

Associated Press, "Study: Immigration Prosecutions Higher, Sentences Longer," *Poughkeepsie [N.Y.] Journal,* July 26, 1999.

Scott Baldauf, "In This City Hall, Official Business Is in Spanish," *Christian Science Monitor,* August 25, 1999.

George Borjas, "Immigration & Welfare," *National Review,* June 16, 1997.

David Brauer, "Twin Cities Radio Station Bows to Hmongs' Pressure," *Chicago Tribune,* November 6, 1998.

Peter Brimelow, "Un-American Activities," *National Review,* June 16, 1997.

William F. Buckley Jr., "Squabbling on the Right," *National Review,* February 24, 1997.

John Cassidy, "The Melting-Pot Myth," *New Yorker,* July 14, 1997.

Linda Chavez, "Debunking the Illegal-Immigrant Welfare Myth," *Denver Post,* March 17, 1999.

Ruth Conniff, "Going Hungry," *Progressive*, July 1998.

Marc Cooper, "The Heartland's Raw Deal," *Nation*, February 3, 1997.

Glynn Custred, "Country Time," *National Review*, June 16, 1997.

Daniela Deane, "Promised Land Yields Bitter Fruit for Some," *USA Today*, October 7, 1998.

FAIR, "Immigration: Kennedy Got It Half Right," *National Review*, June 16, 1997.

"Food Stamps Again for Legal Immigrants," *America*, October 10, 1998.

Charles C. Foster, "Open Our Doors Wider to Needed Workers," *Houston Chronicle*, July 25, 1999.

Ron French and Christopher M. Singer, "Newcomers Challenge Traditional Hamtramck," *Detroit News*, June 14, 1999.

"Give Me—Everybody," *National Review*, December 31, 1997.

Paul Glastris, "The Alien Payoff," *U.S. News & World Report*, May 26, 1997.

Howard Gleckman, "High-Tech Talent: Don't Bolt the Golden Door," *Business Week*, March 16, 1998.

Greg Goldin, "The Greening of Hate," *Nation*, May 18, 1998.

August Gribbin, "Alien Invasion Alarms Arizonans," *Washington Times*, June 7, 1999.

Viva Hardigg, "When Prop. 187 Comes to the Classroom," *U.S. News & World Report*, February 3, 1997.

Susan Headden, "Favor Aliens with Job Skills," *U.S. News & World Report*, December 29, 1997–January 5, 1998.

Thaddeus Herrick, "Spanish Official Language in 'Safe-Haven' Border City," *Houston Chronicle*, August 14, 1999.

"The Khannouchi Case," *Runner's World*, June 1999.

Douglas W. Kmiec, "Gov. Davis Should Do the Right Thing on Prop. 187," *Los Angeles Times*, April 2, 1999.

Claudia Kolker, "Town Speaks the Language of Its People," *Los Angeles Times*, August 13, 1999.

"Legal and Fearful Too," *Los Angeles Times,* June 4, 1997.

Michael Lind, "Hiring from Within," *Mother Jones,* July/August 1998.

Hugo Martin, "Interpreters Give Access to Civic Life—and Raise Assimilation Concerns," *Los Angeles Times,* August 3, 1999.

Abigail McCarthy, "The New Immigrants," *Commonweal,* April 24, 1998.

Scott McConnell, "Americans No More?" *National Review,* December 31, 1997.

Patrick J. McDonnell, "State OKs Prenatal Aid for Immigrants," *Los Angeles Times,* July 27, 1999.

Ramon G. McLeod, "Why Proposed Crackdowns on Immigrants Never Happened," *San Francisco Chronicle,* October 16, 1998.

"Melting Pot Bubbling Along," *Los Angeles Times,* August 2, 1999.

"The Melting Pot Survives," *Economist,* July 3, 1999.

Dan Mihalopoulos, "Growing Beyond the Melting Pot," *St. Louis Post-Dispatch,* May 9, 1999.

John J. Miller, "The Politics of Permanent Immigration," *Reason,* October 1998.

Carol Morello, "Living in Fear on the Border," *USA Today,* July 21, 1999.

"More to Come," *National Review,* October 13, 1997.

Negative Population Growth, Inc., "Why We Must Reduce Immigration from over One Million to 100,000 a Year," *National Review,* June 16, 1997.

Sean Paige, "Raiding Arizona," *Washington Times,* July 26, 1999.

Dick Patrick, "Khannouchi Chases His American Dream," *USA Today,* October 1, 1998.

Chitra Ragavan and Douglas Pasternak, "A Borderline Cop Shop?" *U.S. News & World Report,* July 19, 1999.

Joe Rodriguez, "Welfare Reform and Latinos," *Nieman Reports,* Summer 1999.

Peter D. Salins, "Assimilation, American Style," *Reason,* February 1997.

————, "Towards a New Immigration Policy," *Commentary,* January 1997.

Dick Schneider and Alan Kuper, "Why We Need a Comprehensive U.S. Population Policy," *Sierra,* January/February 1998.

Esther Schrader, "GOP's Muted Response to Welfare Plan Is a Telling Sign of the Times," *Los Angeles Times,* February 8, 1999.

Ronald Steel, "The Bad News," *New Republic,* February 10, 1997.

Dan Stein, "Immigration Is Fueling Poverty Rate," *Los Angeles Times,* July 6, 1999.

Marcus Stern, "Withering Wages," *San Diego Union-Tribune,* August 23, 1999.

Mark Stricherz, "Bill of Wrath," *Nation,* May 11, 1998.

Daniel W. Sutherland, "Identity Crisis," *Reason,* December 1997.

Jamie Trecker, "Regis: Soccer Mercenary U.S. Player Just Became U.S. Citizen," *USA Today,* May 27, 1998.

David Warner, "Reaching the Limit on Worker Visas," *Nation's Business,* August 1998.

Sheba R. Wheeler, "Hmong Parents Strive to Connect," *Denver Post,* November 15, 1998.

Dana Wilkie and Marcus Stern, "America's Immigration Dilemma," *San Diego Union-Tribune,* August 24, 1999.

Gordon Witkin, "One Way, $28,000," *U.S. News & World Report,* April 14, 1997.

Index

abuse, of children, 23

access, to government services, 44–55

advocates, 84–86

Africa, 23

African Americans, 41

Aid to Families with Dependent Children, 47

airports, 67–68

Albanians, 17

army. *See* military

Asia, 23

assembly lines, 61

assimilation, 13–29

asylees (refugees), 78, 81

athletes, 74–76

Australia, 87

balkanization, 13–14

Barton, Flora, 14

beatings, 23

Beck, Roy, 79, 84, 87

Belgium, 16, 19

bilingual education, 22

birth rates, 82, 86

Border Patrol, U.S., 56–58, 62–63, 65, 67, 69, 73

Borjas, George, 40, 54–55

Boxer, Barbara, 66

Brimelow, Peter, 19, 23

Bryson, Bill, 29

Buchanan, Patrick, 18, 65

building maintenance. *See* maintenance

Burtless, Gary, 37

Bush, George W., 36

businesses, created by immigrants, 37

California

adoption of Proposition 187 in, 44–46

costs of immigration in, 46–47

educating children in, 52

Hmong immigrants in, 23

Korean grocers in, 27

labor brokers in, 32

Canada, 19, 87

Central America, 24, 59

Central Valley, 61

Chavez, Linda, 22, 52, 54–55

Chicago, 61
child abuse, 23
China, 59
Chinese immigrants, 25
Chinese New Year, 19
Cincinnati, 27
Cinco de Mayo, 24
citizenship. *See* naturalization
computer programmers, 34
construction, 34, 37
Cook, Adam, 77
costs, of immigration, 46–48
counterfeit documents, 63
Cuba, 78
culture, 23–27

de Mola, Carlos Loret, 20
depletion of resources, 84
detention, 67
Dominicans, 20, 25
Douglas, Arizona, 56–59

Eastern Europe, 59
economic hardships, 10
education. *See* schools
El Cenizo, Texas, 13–15
El Paso, 56–57, 59, 62
Elgin, Illinois, 38
Ellis Island, 26
emergency medical care, 50
engineers, 35
English language, 13–15, 21, 27
environmental concerns, 86
epilepsy, 23
expenses. *See* costs, of immigration

Faircloth, Lauch, 48
family preferences, 78–80
fertility rates, 86
fines, 70
fishermen, 27
Florida, 52
food stamps, 47
foreign languages. *See* languages
France, 16
freeways, 85
Fukuyama, Francis, 16

Gallegly, Elton, 65
Garden City, Kansas, 32
German immigrants, 26
Germany, 16
Gonzales, Rodolfo, 20
government services, 44–55
Gramm, Phil, 49
grocers, 27, 39

Hamtramck, Michigan, 22–23
healers, 23
health care. *See* medical care
high-tech companies, 35, 38
Hispanic Americans, 56
Hmong immigrants, 23–24
Hong Kong, 48
housing, 47
Houston, 34, 37, 61
Huddle, Donald, 35, 37
Hunter, Duncan, 65

identification cards, 71
illegal immigrants, 10, 44–46, 52, 56–74

Illinois, 52
Immigration and Naturalization
  Service. *See* INS
INS (Immigration and
  Naturalization Service), 56,
  59, 65, 67–68, 71
insurance, 31
Iowa, 30
Iowa Beef Processors, 31–32
Italian immigrants, 25–26
Italy, 16

jobs. *See* workers
John F. Kennedy Airport, 67

Keeley, John, 13–14
Khannouchi, Khalid, 75–76

landscaping, 40
languages, 13–15, 21–22,
  26–27
Laos, 23–24
Latin America, 23
layoffs, 32
Lebanon, 19
Lexington, Nebraska, 32
Lind, Michael, 38
Los Angeles, 34, 40, 68
Los Angeles County, 22
Los Angeles Times (newspaper),
  54

Maine, 52
maintenance, 34, 40
marriage, 23
McCarthy, Kevin, 88
meatpackers, 30–34

Medicaid, 47, 54
Medi-Cal, 44, 51
medical care, 23, 46, 50–51
Melting Pot, The (play), 18
Mexico, 24, 56, 59, 67
military, 67–69
Milwaukee, 27
Minnesota, 23, 30

National Academy of Sciences,
  37
National Council of La Raza,
  79
National Guard, 66
national security, 61
naturalization, 74, 76
New Year
  Chinese, 19
  Hmong, 24
New York City, 20, 25, 61,
  67–68
New York State, 27, 37

oath of citizenship, 28
occupational preference, 78, 80
Olympics, 75

penalties, for illegal
  immigrants, 63, 70
point systems, 87–88
political dislocation, 10
population, of United States,
  83–86
preferences, 77–78
prenatal care, 49
privacy, 72
proassimilationists, 21

Proposition 187, 44–46
public housing, 47

reforms in immigration
  policies, 74–90
refugees, 11, 78, 80–82
Regis, David, 74, 76
rejection of assimilation, 19–21
restaurants, 61
restaurant workers, 27
restrictions on immigration, 10
reunification, 78–80
right to privacy, 72
Rodriguez, Rafael, 14
Roosevelt, Theodore, 17, 25
Rotella, Sebastian, 63, 73
Russia, 16, 78

St. Louis, 27
salaries. *See* wages
Salins, Peter D., 16, 20, 25, 73,
  78, 82
San Diego, 56–57, 59, 65, 68
schools, 44–46, 50, 52, 84
Schultz, Tim, 13–14
selling immigration slots,
  88–89
Sierra Club, 86
Simon, Julian, 35, 47, 86
Simon, Laura, 72
Simpson, Alan, 62, 71
Smith, Lamar, 76
Social Security, 47, 50
Soviet Union. *See* Russia
Spanish language, 13, 21, 26
SSI (Supplemental Security
  Income), 48–49

Steel, Ronald, 34–35
Stein, Dan, 47
Storm Lake, Iowa, 30–31
strikes, 32–33
Supplemental Security Income.
  See SSI
sweatshops, 36, 61

Taiwan, 48
taxes, 45, 53
Texas, 27, 32, 52, 84
tradition. *See* culture
traffic, 85

Ukraine, 78
unassimilated immigrants,
  18–19
undocumented aliens. *See*
  illegal immigrants
unemployment, 34, 35
unions, 30, 32
University of Houston, 40–41
urban sprawl, 86
U.S. Army. *See* military
U.S. Border Patrol. *See* Border
  Patrol, U.S.
U.S. Olympic team, 76
Utah, 52

Valentine's Day, 23
values, 23–24
Vance, Larry, 58, 67
Vernez, Georges, 88
Vietnam, 78

wages, 31, 37–41, 52
Wagner, David, 74

Wall Street Journal
  (newspaper), 42
wars, 10
water, 84
Wegerle, Roy, 74
welfare. *See* government
  services
Wilderness Society, 84
Wilson, Pete, 48, 65

Wisconsin, 23
workers, 10, 27, 30–43
work ethic, 36
World Cup, 74, 76
World War I, 26

Yugoslavia, 16, 19

Zangwill, Israel, 18

Picture Credits

ABOUT THE AUTHOR

Stephen Currie is the author of more than twenty books and many magazine articles. Among his nonfiction titles are *Music in the Civil War, Birthday A Day, Problem Play,* and *We Have Marched Together: The Working Children's Crusade.* He is also a first- and second-grade teacher. Currie lives in upstate New York, with his wife, Amity, and two children, Irene and Nicholas.